Life in a Thundering Bay

River Rocks Publishing

Life in a Thundering Bay

Tania L. Saj
Elle Andra-Warner

Copyright © 2007 Tania L. Saj and Elle Andra-Warner
Second Printing, Spring 2008
Third Printing, Fall 2012
Fourth Printing, Summer 2014
Fifth Printing, Winter 2018

All rights reserved. The use of any part of this publication reproduced, transmitted in any form or by any means electronic, mechanical, photocopying, recording or otherwise, or stored in a retrieval system, without the prior written consent of the publisher—or, in the case of photocopying or other reprographic copying, a license from the Canadian Copyright Licensing Agency—is an infringement of the copyright law.

National Library of Canada Cataloguing in Publication

Saj, Tania L.
Andra-Warner, Elle
Life in a Thundering Bay: voices from Thunder Bay's past
Includes bibliography and index.

ISBN 978-0-9782721-0-4
1. Superior, Lake. 2. Ontario, Northern.
I. Title

Printed and bound in Canada by Friesens
Printed on 100% recycled and acid-free paper

ENVIRONMENTAL BENEFITS STATEMENT

River Rocks Publishing saved the following resources by printing the pages of this book on chlorine free paper made with 100% post-consumer waste.

TREES	WATER	ENERGY	SOLID WASTE	GREENHOUSE GASES
6	2,214	4	284	533
FULLY GROWN	GALLONS	MILLION BTUs	POUNDS	POUNDS

Calculations based on research by Environmental Defense and the Paper Task Force.
Manufactured at Friesens Corporation

Published in Canada by River Rocks Publishing
#331 - 1100 Memorial Avenue
Thunder Bay ON P7B 4A3
www.riverrocks.ca

In memory of our grandmother and mother,

REGINA JURIVEE

(1917-1992)

Contents

Introduction **xi**

Life
Canoe Trip to Kakabeka Falls (1873) **3**
Reminiscences of a Vagabond (1883–1884) **16**
The Northern (1887) **45**
The Lost Mother Lode (1926) **52**

Death and Snowstorms
Indian Legend of Loch Lomond (1906) **103**
The Lost Mine of Silver Islet (1922) **109**
The Great Storm (1893) **129**

Thunder
The Legend of Thunder—
How Thunder Bay Obtained its Name (1887) **145**

Epilogue
Place Names in the Vicinity of Fort William (1925) **157**

Index **181**
Bibliography **183**
Photograph and Illustration Credits **184**
Chapter Credits **186**
Acknowledgements **187**

Photographs

Thunder Cape, West Face (1870) **5**
McIntyre Residence (c.1900) **7**
Kakabeka Falls (1872) **13**
Port Arthur (1884) **19**
Port Arthur Post Office (1892) **23**
Buildings in Port Arthur (1889) **28**
Residences in Port Arthur (1889) **29**
Butcher's Boy (1883) **35**
Sailor's Institute (1910) **37**
Marina, Port Arthur (c.1885) **40**
Water Street (1880s) **41**
The Northern (1887) **49**
W.S. Piper (c.1925) **53**
Dog Lake Effigy (c.1925) **59**
Chief Skeet (c.1925) **68**
Mount McKay (1899) **104**
Thunder Cape (1919) **111**
Silver Islet Mine (1880s) **115**
North Shore (c.1909) **117**
Silver Islet Mine (c.1910) **118**
Silver Islet Beach (c.1910) **121**
Dog Sled (1883-84) **125**
Silver Islet Mine (c.1902) **127**
Cumberland Street (1893) **134**
Mary J.L. Black (c.1910) **158**
Prince Arthur (1869) **172**
First C.P.R through train (1886) **174**

Illustrations

Map of Thunder Bay (1870) **xiii**
The 'Algoma' passing Thunder Cape (1870) **47**
Northern Hotel Advertisement (1887) **48**
Ojibway Graves (1857) **63**
Falls on Dog River (1857) **64**
Dog Lake Portage (1857) **71**
Sioux Dress and Moccasins (1860) **83**
Nipigon River (1870) **85**
Tobacco Pipes (1860) **93**
Engraving of Sleeping Giant (1887) **148**
Kakabeka Falls (1870) **164**
Mount McKay (1870) **168**
Red Rock (1870) **169**
Prince Arthur's Landing (1870) **173**
The Dawson Route to Red River (1872) **176**

x

Introduction

The collection of stories before you is the result of our curiosity getting the better of us. It all started one day when we came across a book in the library called *The Eagle of Thunder Cape*, written by W. S. Piper, and published in 1926. The book sounded interesting, and it seemed to take place in Thunder Bay, but neither of us had heard of it before. With so many other books to read, it sat on the bookshelf for awhile, but then, as the due date was fast approaching, the dust was blown off the cover, and the yellowed pages opened. Once opened, we could not put the book down. Why? Well, Piper's book introduced us to a history of Thunder Bay, that, up until then we were largely unaware. For example, we barely knew where Thunder Cape was, had only a vague knowledge of the silver 'rush', and were not familiar with much of the rich Ojibway history of the area. We were used to thinking of Thunder Bay in terms of fur trade history alone.

From that point on, we became avid readers of all things 'Thunder Bay'; moreover, what we found was amazing. This area is rich in stories and fascinating people; we even found epic poems written about the area. Nobody writes epic poems about Thunder Bay today! Upon finding these interesting nuggets, we would share our discoveries with family and friends. We were all surprised to find out how *little* we knew about Thunder Bay, and how *much* there was to know.

Finally, after reading over 100 newspaper articles, books, poems, journal publications, and letters we decided to compile the best of what we had found, and share it beyond the kitchen table. In selecting our choices, we had the following criteria. First, we decided to concentrate on stories that dated back to the earliest days of Port Arthur and Fort William and tried to use primary sources as much as possible, or, as close as we could get. Second, we only selected stories that surprised us, made us laugh, or cringe. Stories that we felt allowed the reader to experience the events, colours, and feelings of a time gone by. We did not want this to be a dry reading of history.

After we had selected our favourite stories, we searched out photographs and illustrations to complement the texts. We looked high and low, and found a treasure trove of remarkable images that most people have likely never seen before. For instance, on page 13 there is a photograph of Kakabeka Falls taken in 1872!

We hope you enjoy this book, and share the stories with your friends and family. In the words of local historian and librarian Mary J.L. Black, we "give it for what it is worth, and because it is all of local interest."

    Tania L. Saj & Elle Andra-Warner
    Thunder Bay, 2007

P.S.: In an effort to not rewrite history, we have not changed the wording of the original texts, except for correcting spelling mistakes, minor grammatical errors, and removing some sections that were not directly relevant to the main body of the text (these sections are indicated by an ellipsis). However, that also means we have not changed several derogatory terms used in the original texts, such as 'Indian', 'Negro', 'Dago', 'Chinaman', 'half-breed', and 'squaw'. We recognize these are unacceptable terms by today's standards, and sincerely hope this does not offend anyone.

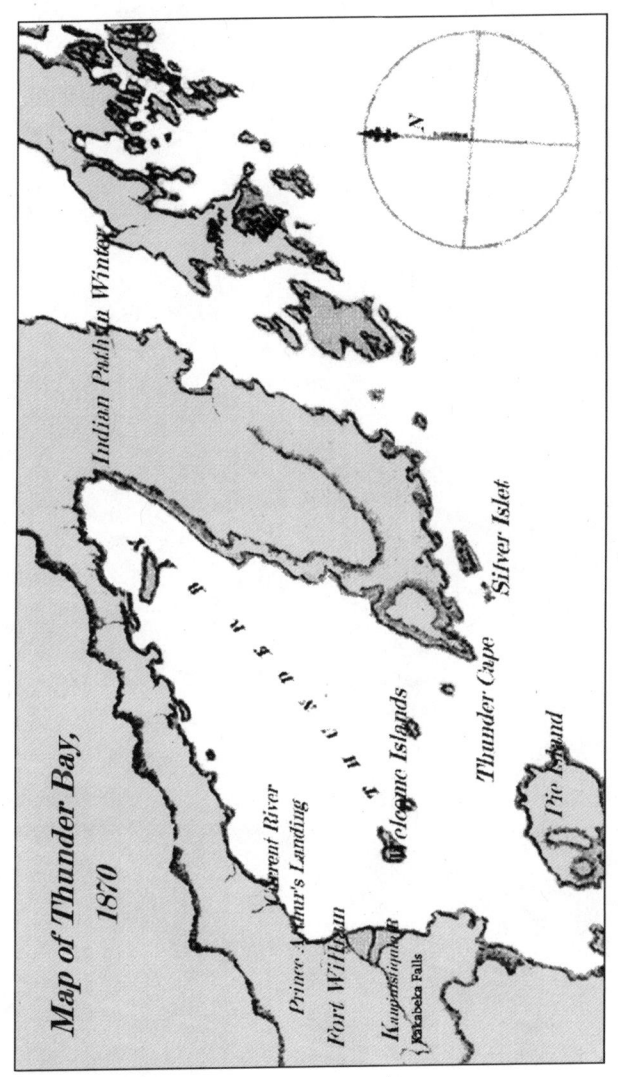

If I were an artist, I would choose Thunder Bay in a storm as the grandest representation of the end of the world.

Catherine Moodie Vickers, 1873

life

Life in a Thundering Bay

CHAPTER ONE

Canoe Trip to Kakabeka Falls (1873)

By Catherine Moodie Vickers

In this wonderful letter, Catherine Moodie Vickers writes to her mother, Susanna Moodie (the famous author of 'Roughing It In The Bush') about her trip to Kakabeka Falls in 1873. Catherine was married to John Vickers, whose family was one of the first to settle in Fort William. We join Catherine as she sails into Thunder Bay, passing the towering Thunder Cape during a terrific storm. Catherine is a natural story-teller—in the 134+ years since this letter was written, we doubt there has been a more striking description of what a thunderstorm over Lake Superior looks like. We follow Catherine as she journeys up the Kaministiquia River, and, we ourselves seem to be seated in the canoe. Keep in mind when you are reading her letter, that Catherine is likely climbing the slate cliffs of Kakabeka Falls in a full-length skirt. In 1902, Catherine donated four hectares of land to the city of Fort William, to create 'Vickers Park', which is still a favourite picnic spot in Thunder Bay.

TLS & EAW

Life in a Thundering Bay

Toronto, Sunday, August 31st, 1873

MY DEAREST MOTHER:

We returned home after a most delightful trip on Wednesday night and I have been so busy settling the house that I could not write sooner. I was so glad to get your letter before starting. I asked Robert to write and tell you how they all were when we were gone, but I have not seen him to see if he did so . . . . We had rather foggy, dull weather on our way up to Lake Superior and after passing Thunder Cape (which is over twelve hundred feet high), and getting into Thunder Bay, **we had a thunder storm which for grandeur I never expect to see surpassed,—the vivid flashes of lightning lighting up the mountains on each side of us** and showing the black waves with their white caps around us on every side; then from all sides of us ribbons of fire ran up the sky in all shapes, more like rockets and fireworks, whilst the thunder leaped from mountain to mountain in a continued roar, like nothing I ever heard before, and followed by a low growl. The lightning I suppose is attracted by the mineral deposits all around Thunder Bay.

Certainly the whole locality is well named. If I were an artist, I would choose Thunder Bay in a storm as the grandest representation of the end of the world. I could not help fancying when I looked over the side of the vessel that I would see old Charon launch his boat from the foot of Thunder Cape.

Thunder Bay would be a magnificent Styx. How I wished

West Cliff, Thunder Cape, 1870

that you could have seen that storm. The Captain who went with me to the extreme bow of the vessel, fearing I think that I would tumble over in my anxiety to see all the storm, said that so many people were afraid of thunder and lightning that he thought that he was the only person that admired lightning, but he had seldom seen it so fine as that night and was so glad to see someone else who liked to watch a storm.

The morning was soft and misty when the little tug came to take us up the river to the Fort and everything was so calm and lovely that it seemed impossible that such a storm had raged the night before. We found the McIntyres all well and Fanny [McIntyre] and her tiny baby there to meet us,—such a lovely creature with such wise blue eyes. Fanny looks younger now than when she was at school. We enjoyed two days seeing our friends at the Fort and dear John [Vickers] was so well—the change did him so much good—that he was anxious I should go to see some of his lots; so Mr. McIntyre suggested that as he had a picked crew of Indians waiting for the Governor of the Hudson's Bay Company, tents, canoes, etc., that I should take them and go up to see the Kakabeka Falls, thirty-three miles above Fort William, the Niagara of the North.

So on Thursday morning at 8:00, Georgie McIntyre and myself took our seats in the middle of one of the grand bark canoes with our blankets under us, for we should have one night under canvas, pillows at our backs and waterproof sheets over us and our effects—John's big picnic basket with provisions for eight—Georgie and myself, John McKellar and Willie Russell and our four brave and tried Indians, the most skillful managers of a canoe in the country, armed with paddles and the iron-tipped poles, the mainstay of our frail bark when we should reach the rapids.

Residence of the McIntyre family (c.1900). The house is still standing on Isabella Street. It was built in 1870.

For the first ten miles from Fort William to Point de Meuron, where steamboat navigation ceases, the river is wide and calm, the morning we started, like a mirror. The men paddled the ten miles without a halt. Just as we came in sight of the point, where Mr. McIntyre has a cottage, the rain, which had been threatening, came down in torrents and we remained a couple of hours, took our dinner, and as the Indians said it would not rain all day we started from there at 2:00 p.m. The rain continued falling at intervals all the afternoon but the wild beauty of the river made us forget it.

Three miles above Point de Meuron at the entrance of the Slate River, where John has a large amount of land, the scenery is beautiful beyond description; on our left Slate River dashing down through the mountains of slate among the beautiful little islands in the Kaministiquia, McKay's mountain behind us, the roaring rapids in front of us, and a beautiful natural meadow on our right with tall elm trees like a plantation, the dense forest rising behind. The greenness of this part of the country is something wonderful. One of the little islands opposite Slate River we could compare to nothing but a salad bowl of fresh lettuce, the green so vivid.

After passing these islands the business of poling the canoe began. Our guide, the old Indian in the bow, stood up and with a careful eye scanned the foaming rapids, then with a few growls and waves of his hand gave the directions to the men after asking anxiously of Georgie if the lady would be afraid. They dislike cowards in a canoe. She assured them that I would not be nervous and when he had gone up the first rapid and I behaved myself they testified their approval by nods and grunts and I rewarded them by glasses of whiskey, tin cups I should say.

Never did men require or deserve refreshment more. The fatigue is immense propelling a canoe, so heavily laden, by main strength up those roaring rapids with short stretches of paddling.

The rapids continue for twenty miles, each one more beautiful than the last and more dangerous to ascend. Mr. McIntyre told the men to take me as much as possible in the canoe if I were not afraid, so at all the worst passages the guide and steersman remained in the canoe with Georgie and me, the gentlemen and the other Indians walking, the Indians carrying the baggage.

The drawing of the canoe between the rocks and waves is the most exciting thing I ever witnessed. Once in a while you feel the poles slip and the canoe is carried many yards down stream, then a sudden dart across the river to some little islet for safety whilst our boatmen wiped their streaming faces and recovered breath, then a fresh tug with the wild stream. I can hardly believe it now it is over that I was so calm and enjoyed the combat with those waters,—only that thin bark between me and instant death, for no one could stand a moment or even swim across those rapids, as we saw by the efforts made by a noble black Eskimo dog belonging to one of our men who had to run along the shore for miles to safe swimming places,—such a noble brute, who called to his master from the high banks first on one side, then the other, sometimes behind us then far ahead.

At 7:00 p.m. we came to the camping ground, just seven miles below the falls. It was just dark and it seemed a strange place to sleep, the grass and trees wet as possible but the men soon trampled down the grass, lighted a fire, and pulled wet boughs for our beds, spread the waterproofs, made the beds, and pitched the tents, whilst Georgie and I laid the tablecloth beside the fire and prepared the meal.

Water was soon boiled in the tea kettle, the tea made and the Indians' pork fried and cake baked. At half-past eight we shut up our tent and changing our clothing for dressing gowns and slippers and after praying in the wilderness for the dear ones at home settled ourselves to sleep. The crackling of the fire kept me awake some time, the roaring of the rapids, then the snoring of the gentlemen in the next tent, but at last all nature was still and we slept soundly until called at 7:00 a.m.

Oh but the waking was cold!

The quick early breakfast did not warm us but a bright glorious sunrise did. Such a morning on such a lovely river; the dew and rain drops sparkling on the trees and grass, the wild convolvulus and wild hops festooning the trees and gay flowers. **I never saw before the red rocks in the river looking like lions and whales.**

The rapids become more rapid, the land higher on each side and by the great roar we knew that we were not far from one of nature's greatest wonders. The sun shines brighter and every minute great patches of white foam pass us. The beauty of that morning repaid us for the fatigue of the long journey, our damp clothes and cramped feet, to say nothing of fly bites which we knew were on our faces, hands and bleeding necks, but who could wear a veil or other protection in such a scene.

At 8:00 a.m., after severe work, our men land us safely at the portage, about a mile below the falls, which are hidden by high rocks. They spread our tents and bedding to dry and insist upon our taking a proper breakfast. Georgie and I help with the table but are too impatient to see the falls to eat. Georgie has been twice there before but was as anxious as myself. After breakfast we leave two men to clear up, wash our bedding, etc.

No living creature there but flies and fishes. With the canoe light we once more go into the rapids and a few vigorous efforts of our guide and steersman puts us past the projecting rocks. I shall never forget my feelings. There before us was the most glorious sight mortal eye could see.

Gilded and burnished by the morning sun and the great current of water came rushing down nearly two hundred feet, the whole breadth of the river, no island or stone to break the outline—one pure torrent of snow-white foam, not clear or crystalline, but like a continuous mass of cream. As it reaches the rapids below it breaks over the rocks which, from the quantity of iron in the neighbourhood, are bright red. The water in a glass is the colour of brandy or sherry wine so you may imagine what it is when the sun shines on those stones. There is a little island formed originally no doubt by the gravel and stones carried down by the river but now covered by a few birches, dogwood and young cherry trees, moss and wild vines, just a little footing I may say, and here we landed so we could look our fill. As we walked we were in the loveliest rainbow—the stones, the trees, everything gloriously coloured with it. Such a fairy island, such shabby folks, all gilded by that rainbow—it seemed magic. We were wet then with the spray but never thought of it.

Looking from the island the falls were directly in front of us, a high cliff of iron and slate on our right hand with giant trees which seemed in the clouds; on our left a steep mountain, or rather two, one above the other covered with moss, so green that the eye could hardly look at it, the lower hill quite round on top without trees or shrubs, the upper one thickly wooded with cedar and tamarack from which hung long grey moss—grey-bearded trees with lovely moss all over the rocks; behind us the roaring rapids. I wish I could paint the picture for you with your fat old daughter all ragged and rumpled, looking at it with the tears streaming down her cheeks, our Indians leaning on their poles, silent and still.

We stayed an hour, then returned to the camp and climbed the mountain from the back and walked along the edge of the highest mountain, looking down into the shining abyss. When there, by careful climbing, we find deep, natural steps in the slate rock and we go down about half the height of the falls and look up and down and into their beauties, again drenched with spray and waters of the actual falls washing our feet.

After the poor human vanity of scratching our names on the rocks, we climb back to the summit of the mountain and gather mosses and that lovely flower which seems to grow wild only in sight of rushing water, the columbine, so fragile and lovely.

I shall never forget my feelings. There before us was the most glorious sight mortal eye could see.

Kakabeka Falls, 1872

We stumble our way down over broken trees and rocks, slippery mosses, and millions of pigeon berries, blue berries and raspberries where there are neither humans nor birds to gather them; back once more to camp, our shoes worn out, our faces one mass of blood, our clothes in rags and tatters, but happy and satisfied and actually hungry. At 2:00 p.m. we leave our camp and turn our looks upon a scene which I do not think it likely I shall ever see in the flesh again, but to be remembered and thought of so long as I have the heart to admire God's wonderful works.

I shall be satisfied for my children to see them and think that I actually had courage and strength to climb those rocks and worship at nature's shrine, before it and they were marred by the hand of man—no taverns or curiosity shops or railways, no steam whistle to bring one down to everyday life.

Our journey down the rapids was quick, exciting work. Four hours brought us back to the first mark of civilization—in Canada, the sawlog. Two hours' steady paddling and we see the sun set on old McKay's red sides reflected in the still river. The mountain looks like Windsor Castle illuminated.

We now meet canoes and boats and see the lights in the little log houses at the Catholic Mission, and 8:00 p.m., Friday August 22nd, land safely at the Fort. Good Mrs. McIntyre and Victor are set at the wharf to meet us, dear Papa getting very uneasy as it is so late. We eat a good tea, take off our old clothes, go to sleep and are all right next day, excepting the horrid fly bites which are not well yet. Saturday we see our friends and pack up; Sunday we say farewell, and to-night just a week from them.

I have scribbled all this just for your amusement and have not told one-half. When you come up I will tell you all the rest. The children are never tired hearing my adventures and consider me a great traveller. I brought home some trophies in the way of stones, moss, etc. I must stop now. It has struck 12:00 and all are in bed asleep. I fear you will not be able to read all this scrawl. Give my love to Aunt Cherry, Katie and all friends, and believe me as ever your loving daughter.

CHAPTER TWO

Reminiscences of a Vagabond (1883–1884)

By Fred M. DelaFosse

This is an extraordinary personal account of Port Arthur in the 1880s. DelaFosse was a 'remittance man'; a remittance man was a traveller, a voluntary ex-patriot, who relied on money sent from home for his travels. We pick up DelaFosse's story as he and his travelling companion, Hall, are making their way from Winnipeg to Fort William then Port Arthur to look for work. DelaFosse's narrative brings to life the growing pains of Port Arthur in the late 1800s. Never one to shy away from adventure, or a fight, DelaFosse introduces us to the rough and tumble world of the lumber camp (and delivering newspapers), as well as picnics on the Welcome Islands, and socials in the houses of upper class families. Lucky for us, he seems to have left no stone unturned and introduces us to a fascinating host of characters. However, his candid description of 'turning upside down' a Chinese laundromat reminds us that racism was also a part of this history.

TLS & EAW

I am not really a vagabond, although for the space of a year and a half I deliberately cut loose from the hum-drum existence of life in the backwoods in order to see something of the world outside .... I am not ashamed to say that I was a remittance man and that I spent all my money, because it was one of the best things that ever happened to me as it forced me to rely on my own resources at an age when I was forceful enough to strike out and do something ....

It would take too long and has nothing to do with the particular phase of my life and adventures which I am recalling to give an extended account of the manner in which I reached Port Arthur. [We applied] at the C.P.R. offices for work down the line ... [and] were given employment, and free passes to get to our destination, at the Plot, now Fort William .... We agreed that we could make the 75 cents do till we got to Fort William and that by purchasing that worth of gingerbread and washing down our meal with water we would feel the equal of the wealthiest in the land ....We managed to keep body and soul together with the gingerbread and when we got to our destination at 'The Plot', as Fort William was called, we were told to shovel coal on the C.P.R. trucks, and advised to board at the Neebing House, a big white-painted wooden structure, standing close to the banks of the Kaministiquia River.

That was really my first introduction to the truly seamy side of life. The beds were beyond measure filthy, and the company was worse. Amongst an agglomeration of Swedes, Russians, Negroes, Dagos and out-at-elbows Englishmen, Hall [his travelling companion] and I soon found our lot was not a happy one.

After two days heavy shovelling on the trucks my right hand developed a felon and I had to rely on Hall to lend me money enough to keep going till I was well again.

That was really my first introduction to the truly seamy side of life.

Port Arthur, 1884

He obtained work for the two of us in a cordwood camp run by Graham and Horn steamboat agents and wood merchants and after a few days helping in the kitchen I went into the woods and started chopping wood. I was adept at chopping as I had already had three years or more experience of it in Parry Sound so it was not hard for me to earn enough to pay Hall back what I owed him and pay my board bill besides.

We put in a strenuous time in the camp as the choppers were an unruly outfit and would fight at the drop of a hat. I had an early experience of this when I got into trouble with a man who had stolen my socks. They were the only pair I possessed and I had deposited them under the stove to dry when I came in from work at night. When I looked for them I found them covering the pedal extremities of a giant named Jim McGrath. Not to enter too closely into details I got back my socks, but only because Mr. McGrath was so astonished at my hardihood in bearding him that after throwing me over his head on to the red-hot stove (he was the champion wrestler of the neighbourhood) he put me on my feet and handed me over the socks.

"Young man," he remarked, "You've took me when I'm feelin' good-natured; if you'd took me when I was feelin' real ugly I'd have knocked the daylights out of you.—Here's yer socks." As I was only anxious to regain my belongings, I was quite pleased when he returned them. He always took my side afterwards, and helped me out of many a tight place with the other ruffians in the camp.

We managed to put in the winter fairly comfortably and then, thinking we would better our condition, hired further up the river to chop wood for Sheriff Carpenter. As my memories of Sheriff Carpenter and of his son are not particularly pleasant ones I shall only say enough to remark that both Hall and I were very pleased when we bade that gentleman and his enterprising son farewell. We were both compelled to carry our trunks down the line towards Port Arthur and seek another boarding-house as the Sheriff, genial gentleman, had told us that we needn't hope to pass the night in his establishment seeing that we had thought fit to give warning and we were therefore no longer in his employ.

I can see ourselves now, each carrying a trunk on his back, wending our way down the road to Port Arthur looking anxiously for any sign of a boarding house to rest our tired bones.

Ten o'clock at night is scarcely a propitious time for seeking an abode and we found ourselves compelled to pass the night sitting on our trunks by the side of the road, sleeping as well as we could in that uncomfortable position. Hall was getting pretty well fed up with this vagabonding and yearned for home and a bath.

He said to me, "Look here, DelaFosse, aren't we two blazing idiots to be voluntarily cutting ourselves adrift from civilization in order to see how the other half lives? As soon as I get to Port Arthur I'm going to write for money to go home."

I was more than half inclined to agree with him but the lust for adventure was strong within me and I told him that though I would be sorry to part company with him I intended to put in one year at any rate before I returned to the backwoods.

We trudged into Port Arthur next morning and with what little money we possessed we purchased bucksaws and saw-horses and started soliciting jobs in the backyards of the wealthier residents. By nightfall we had managed to strike employment and also to gain an entrance into a passably clean boarding house, not one of the sort that charged ten dollars a week but clean and cheap nevertheless.

We used to sally out every morning with our sawhorses on our shoulders and at the end of a few weeks were fairly conversant with the back premises of the houses of the Port Arthur gentry. But this was Hall's expiring effort. He wrote as he had threatened to do and on receiving money from home took the first steamer back to his people. We parted from each other with regret. He had been a good friend to me and possibly I had been a fairly good friend to him, but it was hard work saying good-bye to him. Henceforth I was thrown entirely on my own resources, and in order to make assurance doubly sure that I should have to work in order to live I deliberately sent home a Letter of Credit for £25 which a compassionate uncle had remitted to me from England. I sometimes felt sorry that I had succumed to such a fit of exuberant self-reliance. However, as events turned out, such a token of independence did me good with the powers at home. My first act after bidding good-bye to Hall was to hunt around for something more elevating and remunerative than sawing wood.

I had always had a penchant for writing and immediately on my arrival in Port Arthur got busy and indited one or two poems for the periodical of that day, the *Port Arthur Sentinel*. They were accepted, with many thanks and no cash but through their agency I became acquainted with Mr. Stilwell, an Englishman, who was then owner or editor of the paper. I shall never forget my first meeting with that gentleman. He had been pointed out to me as editor of the paper so I made bold, one day, when I had my sawhorse on my shoulder to accost him and ask if he could oblige me with some literary

Post Office at the corner of Red River Road and Court Street, 1892

work. After talking a few minutes he was kind enough to say, "I see that you are an Englishman, like myself, and of course I am always anxious to help a fellow-country man; in this case more particuarly so as I see that you are a man who has not been brought up to saw wood. Come round to my office at 5 p.m. and I shall have a literary job for you."

I thanked him heartily, and he said with a magnificent gesture, "Don't mention it, my dear fellow, pray don't mention it—it will be one of the happiest days of my life if by any means in my power I have been able to help a man in distress."

I was in no distress but I did not think it necessary to enlarge on that point and hastened to bedeck myself in all the finery I possessed in order to present myself in a becoming manner at the office of the paper. Having nothing much beyond a clean collar and a dirty shirt and trousers, I went the round of my friends and managed by dint of great effort to collect together a complete outfit. It was a variegated assortment. A pair of trousers from a man called Gavey, who was 6 feet 5 and abnormally thin, a shirt from a man who took a 16 collar and a red tie, brand new, from a freckle-faced youth lately arrived from Ireland.

When I look back at that time I see elements of humour in it, but I was in a very serious mood and most strongly imbued with a sense of my importance when I arrived at the office in my borrowed plummage.

I waited patiently and after about fifteen minutes, Stilwell came into the room and saw me sitting in his editorial chair.

"What the?—" he exclaimed, but recognizing the occupant of his sanctum, he added, "Oh, yes, DelaFosse, you've come for that job haven't you?" I purred in a pleased manner that I had.

"Well," he said, "I am afraid that you won't find much in it at first but you know, one has always to begin at the beginning and climb upwards to the stars. That's the way I had to do it and look at me now," and he puffed his portly frame till he resembled a barrel.

"Now," he continued, "what I want you to do is to carry these papers round town. The pay won't be much as we are not able to pay as much as we would like but there is always a chance for a raise for a good man." I was aghast—all my dreams of blossoming out as an editor and influencing the world faded out into the ewigkeit and it was with a crestfallen look and humble voice that I asked him how much there was in the job.

"Well," he remarked, "seeing that you are not like some of the useless young devils I've had round me lately, I'll make it worth your while and say $8 a month, without board." My first impulse was to tell Mr. Stilwell that his overwhelming generosity was too much for me and that I could not possibly bring myself to accept such a munificent offer but on second thought, seized with the spirit of adventure and seeing that I knew nobody, I said, "Well, I'll try it for a week anyhow—give us the papers."

I only lasted one night. In the course of my round I had to enter a grocery store, and had laid the paper on the counter and was just turning to go out when the clerk espied me and called out, "Say, young feller, is that the Sentinel?" I blandly replied that it was.

"I've a blamed good mind to kick you," the youth shouted, "that paper hasn't been delivered for six weeks past."

"Oh, indeed!" I replied.

"Get out of here," he cried, *"and don't you sauce me!"*

"I'm not going to get out of here," I answered, "until I have found out whether you can kick me out."

There were no more papers delivered that night. In less time than it takes to write, we were having a rough and tumble fight on the floor and the evening's edition was scattered about in every portion of it. First one, then the other would be on top and we rolled about and mauled each other in the most approved style of ruffianism.

Finally, we rolled right out of the store into the street and fought in the gutter. In about five seconds a howling mob had collected and I was told afterwards that amongst them was the Chief of Police, an Irishman of the name of Burke, who was enjoying the spectacle as much as anybody. It was only when an old lady came along and tapped him on the shoulder and told him that he ought to be ashamed of himself, allowing such goings on that he took a hand in the game and with the aid of one or two bystanders dragged us apart. He was a fine chap, was Burke; all he said when we were separated was, "Get away as quick as you can."

We took him at his word—the clerk vanished into the store and I sneaked up a bye street to my humble lodging. We were a terrible sight, both of us, covered with mud and gore and our clothing ruined. I am happy to say that when brighter days dawned for me I was able to make the acquaintance of that clerk and found him not such a bad fellow after all.

Next morning I went to Stilwell and told him that I resigned the job. I said that I was not yet fully qualified to fight in the prize ring and that when I did I would do it under different auspices. What he needed was a John L. Sullivan on the staff. I sent him a piece of verse afterwards which he did not publish, to emphasize my ideas on the subject.

I returned to my sawing, finding it infinitely more lucrative and free from strife. I had an uneasy time of it with my friends when I had to inform them of the damage to their clothing. They were inclined to be nasty about it and said unkind things and wondered when I would be able to make good the injury. However, I was able to pay them back in a short time as another letter of credit happened along and I was able to indemnify them.

After some months of buck-sawing I had the good fortune to meet a Mr. Furlong, a Land Surveyor, who was interested in surveying mining locations and having made known to him my desire to obtain a change of employment he very kindly offered me a place with him on his surveying staff. This proved to be the end of my financial worries for he paid me $3 a day, one dollar more than any of the rest were getting owing to the fact that I was an expert chopper, which was what he was in need of.

But my adventures in Port Arthur were by no means over. I had made friends with a Mr. Romaine Winans, a gentleman of roving proclivities with a wide knowledge of liquors, who, like myself, was on his beam sides and taking whatever job came into view. We lived together in a little lodging house where we hired a bedroom and took our meals whenever it pleased us. Winans sometimes came with us on short surveys, if he was fortunate enough to be in a healthy condition when we started on our treks, but as he so often celebrated the good luck of landing a job by getting drunk the night before we often had to go off without him.

We often left poor Winans at home. We were away about two weeks engaged on a survey in the vicinity of the Rabbit Mountain Silver Mine, which was owned by a half-breed of the name of Oliver Daunais, under whose auspices the party was engaged in making further locations. Daunais was with us and so was his father-in-law, an Indian chief, a fine old man of the name of Cheeataw, a Chippewa. We had a fairly strenuous time on that survey, and I will never forget having to carry a man on my back 7½ miles through the woods to the nearest camp. He had severed an artery with an axe . . . .

My memories are very keen of that particular survey because on my return I took my washing to a Chinaman to get washed[1]. He handed me a piece of paper with some hieroglyphics on it and I went home happy. At the end of the week I went for my clothing and was handed back a handkerchief and a collar which did not belong to me. As the Chinaman could not talk a word of English and I was equally ignorant of Chinese our palaver came to nothing and I invoked the aid of my friend the Chief of Police in the discussion.

Life in a Thundering Bay

Port Arthur, 1889 1- McGillis Block 2- Ray St & Co's Bank 3- Flaherty Block and Bodega Hotel 4- Fire Hall 5- Cameron St 6- Ontario Bank, Ray's Block 7- Burk Block 8- Bawlf Block 9- Cordingly Block

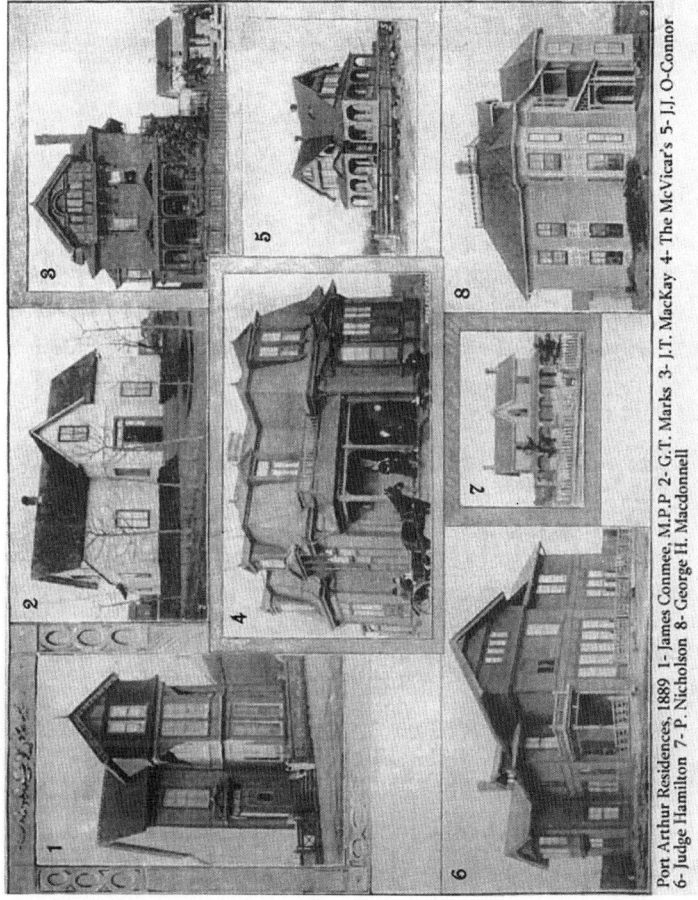

Port Arthur Residences, 1889 1- James Conmee, M.P.P. 2- G.T. Marks 3- J.T. MacKay 4- The McVicar's 5- J.J. O'Connor 6- Judge Hamilton 7- P. Nicholson 8- George H. Macdonnell

Nothing came to that either and the Chief told me that I had better be content and not sue him as nobody could understand the man anyway. On my remarking that I didn't see why a Chinaman should be allowed to go scot free after virtually robbing a man, he said pleasantly that the best thing I could do was to take it out on his hide and he guessed the magistrate would treat the thing leniently.

Common assault was so common in those days, owing to the squabbles amongst the navvies [unskilled labourers] that a mere misunderstanding in which a Chinaman might get his head broken was looked upon as a joke; a good thing for the Chinaman in showing him that he was in a free country. He could steal your clothes and get off with them and you could on the other hand, retaliate by breaking his head and get off with that.

I went home in a very dejected frame of mind and poured out my woes into Winans' sympathetic ear.

"Leave it to me, old man," he observed, "I'm not going to see you stuck—just watch your uncle." He went out and I settled down in a chair to cogitate over the matter.

In about half an hour an emissary from the Police Court presented himself at the door and handed me a note. It proved to be from Winans, telling me that he had been landed in jail for turning the Chinaman's laundry upside down and turning the Chinaman himself into the road. He asked me to come and provide bail for him so that he might be able to get home and have his tea in peace.

I went to the Police Court, and didn't have much trouble in arranging with my friend the Chief to let Winans out of the cells. He appeared next morning before the magistrate and was let off with a small fine. In speaking to me about his experience at the laundry, he said that he had got so tired of trying to make the Chinaman understand what he wanted that he simply took him by the scruff of the neck and threw him out of doors and then proceeded to gather up such articles of attire as he thought I might require in order to make good my loss. As these would have been the property of various unknown individuals it seemed hardly the proper method of procedure. However, the matter blew over but I never got my clothes back again.

A very interesting man whom I met on my varied excursions into the woods was a Captain Walpole Roland[2], a retired English army officer. He was a friend of Furlong's and used to be of some service to him in an engineering capacity. At that time Captain Roland was a man of about fifty-five years of age, slight and sinewy, and with a decided taste for strong drink. He had had many hairbreadth escapes in the wilds, among others, he had been the sole survivor of a landslide in the vicinity of James Bay. He had also had a narrow escape from death in attempting to cross from Red Rock to the mainland, a feat which he accomplished successfully, but his dog was drowned. . . .

Another good friend of mine was George McVicar, whose death I noticed in the papers a few years ago. He was an old-timer at Port Arthur and I think was a near connection of the Moberly family or of the McKellars. Then there were Russell, the land surveyor, and Frank and Tom Keefer, lawyers, and Wink, also a lawyer, Munro, another lawyer, and Neil McDougall, a well known resident of the town. I remember a dance at his mother's house and going in a pair of trousers and a dress coat borrowed from my 6 foot 5 friend Gavey. It was an awful ordeal as when I entered the room to make my bow to Mrs. McDougall, the strain proved too much for my attire and I had to spend the rest of the evening with my back studiously kept to the wall, for fear of exhibiting the damage done to my unmentionables. As a wallflower, I proved a success for I talked to two or three ladies who seemed astonishingly lacking in partners, and apparently glad to have someone to talk to. It was a great night.

My memories of Neil McDougall and of Munro are most vividly connected with a certain First of July celebration when all sorts of sports were arranged for the proper observance of the day. It has to be remembered that at that time Port Arthur was a very differently constituted place from what it is today. The town was simply over-run with navvies as the C.P.R. was in the course of construction. The bars were wide open and there was a very considerable sprinkling of desperate characters[3]. It can easily be imagined, therefore, that a First of July celebration was altogether likely to be a very lively observance. Amongst the sports on the program was a swimming race from dock to dock and back again, and there were also rowing and canoe races. The docks were simply jammed with navvies and other onlookers . . . .

Amongst my other recollections of Port Arthur is a very vivid one of a man called Barrett with whom I used to room in a little dwelling on Water Street. He was a terrible drinker and there were all sorts of pledges pinned up on the wall in our room, which poor Barrett had taken at various times and had systematically broken. He was in the throes of another effort to ban drink when I met him and I can remember so well when I first entered his room being struck with the apparent firmness of will he evinced in regard to topping. I asked him to have a drink from a bottle in my possession but he cried in a theatrical manner, "Avaunt, I never take the cursed stuff." Then he pointed to the pledges on the wall.

"Don't tempt me, my friend," he said, "don't tempt me."

I put the bottle away and after a few minutes Barrett called to me.

"I'm feeling very weak and tired today. Do you know, a little drop of that cordial of yours would do me no harm."

"Remember your pledge," I said, and Barrett subsided.

We went to bed and in the middle of the night I was awakened by the sound of something gurgling from a bottle. I sat up, lit the lamp, and discovered Barrett gulping down a generous draught of whiskey from a bottle he had secreted under his pillow.

Of course, the end of that poor chap was disastrous. I think I am right in saying that he came to his end by jumping off the taffrail of the Butcher's Boy, a vessel owned by a man named Smith, who was engaged in providing meat supplies for the navvies on the different contracts down the line.

A man named Healey used to keep the Shuniah House[4], a hotel situated a short distance above Water Street, on a street leading to the Ridge, where a number of us young English good-for-nothings used to assemble at night to sing songs and engage in other festive doings. Healy died and his widow started a boarding house. A friend of mine, named Massey, and myself, took rooms there and stayed for a considerable time.

One of the most embarrassing experiences I ever had occurred in that boarding house. Surveys of mining locations used to take me away from Port Arthur for two or three weeks at a time and I was in the habit of coming back to the boarding house at all hours of the day or night.

Massey had occupied his room for months and as we were very close friends we used to make free of each other's belongings and walk in to greet each other in a thoroughly unceremonious manner.

"Do you know, a little drop of that cordial of yours would do me no harm."

"Butchers Boy" at McKellar's Harbor

Butcher's Boy, 1883.

On one such occasion, when I had been absent about three weeks I reached Port Arthur about three o'clock in the morning and, as was my custom, went straight to Massey's room. I tiptoed in and wishing to give him a good scare I reached out and caught what I thought was Massey's hair and gave it a hearty pull.

"Wake up," I said. But to my horror, an ear-piercing yell from a woman rang out on the night air.

They had changed Massey's sleeping apartment during my absence and on this particular night a married couple was in possession of it. The whole house was roused and I had an awkward time explaining my mistake. Luckily the aggrieved couple were also friends of mine and everything was forgiven. But I very much doubt if the lady in question will ever forget the fright she received on that night.

I could ramble on at pretty considerable length and tell a number of exciting experiences, humourous and otherwise but it is almost with a feeling of sadness that the mind reverts to those days.

One of the saddest of all experiences was when the Northern Hotel was burnt to the ground[5], I shall always remember that. One poor fellow, whom I had known, (I forget his name), a traveller for the firm of Cascaden and Peck of Winnipeg, had escaped and was out in the street watching the progress of the fire, when he remembered that he had left some money belonging to his employers in his room. He rushed back but was caught by the falling in of the roof, and burnt to death. It was a terrible ending.

Another memory that looms up is of an attempt made one night by a half-starved young man to sandbag me. If he had been successful he would have secured the princely sum of one dollar which I had earned that day by buck-sawing, but he was

Sailor's Institute on Water Street, 1910

The bars were wide open and there was a very considerable sprinkling of desperate characters...

unsuccessful and I managed to keep my dollar. He told me when I let him go that he had been without food for four days and was driven to desperation. I met him next morning at the corner of the street by Tom Marks' store [corner of Red River Road and Water Street] and he was so shamefaced that he couldn't look me in the face....

One funny thing that happened was when one fine day in summer a large party of young men and women started out for the Welcome Islands on a picnic. Whilst they were enjoying themselves a storm came up and the whole party were marooned for the night on one of the islands, and had to shelter themselves as best they could. Possibly some of the older residents may remember that episode. There were many nervous parents in Port Arthur that night, anxious for the safety of their sons and daughters.

Our surveying trips took us into strange places. One of our engagements was to survey the stone at Thunder Cape as a gentleman from London, owner of one of the papers there, had come to the conclusion that it was good for paving stones. The Bay was covered with ice and the party started off to trek across to the Cape. I forget exactly how many miles it is distant from Port Arthur, but I know that it took us the best part of the day getting across as we had to make wide detours owing to huge cracks in the ice. It was glare ice at that and mighty hard to keep one's feet on it. It was very cold weather and as we had no tents, the entire party made the best of things and built a roaring fire, curled up in their Hudson's Bay blankets and went to sleep under the starry sky....

Our peregrinations sometimes took us far afield. In one of our trips we paddled and portaged for miles up the Nipigon River—a wonderful river, filled with speckled trout. We were within ten or twelve miles of Nipigon Lake. I can well remember that our party was caught by Mr. Ronison, the resident Church of England clergyman at the mission of Nipigon, near Red Rock, and treated to a sermon of more than an hour's duration. It was raining but that mattered nothing to the zealous clergyman. He stood it and made us all stand it too . . . .

A very interesting character whom I met at Port Arthur was an Englishman who went by the name of Dynamite Sutton. He was a gentleman, working for his living, like ourselves, but his specialty was one that none of us would have cared to engage in. He was engaged to cart dynamite to the various contracts along the line. It didn't matter to Sutton how rough the road was. The way in which he would jog up and down the declivities was a caution. I never heard of his being blown up in an explosion. Fortune in this case favoured the brave. Another friend of mine was not so fortunate. He invited me to spend the evening with him in his shack in the hills beyond Silver Current. I was unable to go and it was just as well. Some nitro-glycerine which he was thawing out at the stove exploded and sent him and his shack into widely scattered portions of adjoining townships.

The last survey in which I was engaged was in the vicinity of Jackfish Bay. We were to survey some copper and zinc locations there and part of our work consisted in having to carry out 160 pounds of quartz apiece on our backs to the lakeshore for transhipment to Port Arthur for the purpose of having it assayed. I have carried rough weights in my time but that particular load was the worst I ever carried. Three miles through the Lake Superior woods, over boulders, down precipices and across deep ravines, without once laying down the burden taxed one's strength to the utmost. At the end of it we were so exhausted that to a man each bought a bottle of

Marina, Port Arthur. c.1885. The Northern Hotel is facing the waterfront. The white building on the right is Thomas Marks' store.

Thomas Marks' Store on Water Street, 1880s. The Northern Hotel is the building in the distance with the verandah.

Northrop and Lyman's Vegetable Dyspeptic Cure at the local railway store and finished it to the last drop. Perhaps it is needless to say that it nearly finished us ....

The day came when I found I had my fill of adventure and hardship. It had proved a very useful experience. I had gone out to see the world in the rough and found it rougher even than I had expected .... I had started in with an overweening pride of my nationality and in the belief that an Englishman was the superior of any other creature on earth. I had discovered ... that even in the outer ranges of civilization, there was being reared a race of men who could hold their own in the company of Englishmen or anyone else. I returned home a chastened individual.

Notes

[1] This is probably the laundry owned by Hem Lee on Pearl Street along the waterfront by the Northern Hotel, as described by local historian Russell Brown in *Thunder Bay's People.*

[2] We meet the adventuresome Captain Roland again in Chapters *Three* and *Eight*

[3] Port Arthur was a drinking man's town. We stumbled upon an undated and anonymous article titled, *Port Arthur was a Wonderful Place for Thirsty Homo Sapiens in 1884,* which tallies the number of drinking establishments in town: "At that time there were no less than 36 licensed hotels, 4 unlicensed hotels, 2 wholesale liquor stores, and 5 retail liquor stores besides 10 well-known blind pigs and several others known to

special patrons only. Not counting the blind pigs, there were 43 outlets for the purchase of intoxicating liquors or approximately 1 outlet for every 25 inhabitants of the town at that time."

[4] The Shuniah House is also described in the above-mentioned article (*Port Arthur was a Wonderful Place for Thirsty Homo Sapiens in 1884*). The anonymous author writes:

"In 1884, the Algoma Hotel was known as the Shuniah House. It was built and owned first by Merrill and Cameron. At the death of Mr. Merrill, the ownership passed to his son John Merrill and his son-in-law Geo. Hodder under the firm name of Merrill and Hodder who renamed it the Algoma Hotel. The building occupied the site of the present Metropolitan Block and faced Lorne Street. George Hodder managed the hotel until his retirement when the property was purchased by the Metropolitan Stores and the hotel was torn down. The Shuniah was a home away from home for a number of prominent personalities over the years. James Oliver Curwood of Owasso, Michigan wrote *God's Country and The Woman*, a novel written around the Nipigon country while he was a paying guest at the hotel in 1905. Another prominent personality who lived at the Shuniah during his sojourn in Port Arthur, was Bob Edwards, the well-known owner and editor of the controversial *Calgary Eye-Opener*, who, for reasons better known to himself and some of the citizens of Calgary, was forced to vacate Calgary, after his publishing plant was wrecked by irate citizens in 1911. His *Eye-Opener* was printed by the *Port Arthur Daily News* on Lorne Street during 1912."

[5] DelaFosse must have meant the Queen's Hotel on Water Street. It burnt down in 1884, and the Northern Hotel was built on the same spot later that year. The gentleman who died was named William MacPherson, he worked for the Cascaden and Peck Company of Winnipeg. In *A History of Thunder Bay*, Joseph M. Mauro, describes MacPherson's death: "When nothing remained of the Hotel but a heap of red, intensely hot ashes, his body was discovered near the road. 'In close proximity lay the lock of the room which the deceased occupied, in which was the key, being number (19). Close by a gold Elgin watch, with the outside case partly melted, was picked up . . .' One man remarked, 'Poor Mac; everybody was a friend of his and he was everybody's friend.'"

CHAPTER THREE

The Northern, the Finest Hotel in Canada West of Toronto—Appreciated Enterprise (1887)

By Captain Walpole Roland

Captain Roland's description of the Northern Hotel makes one wish they were a 19th century tourist. Imagine a hotel in Thunder Bay with a writing room, grand staircase, reading room, and marble countertops in the washroom. The Northern Hotel was built in 1884 on the corner of Water and Park Streets, facing the Marina. In 1904, Frank Mariaggi bought the Northern and renamed it the Mariaggi Hotel (rumours from the prohibition era suggest it may have been a liquor smuggling point for the Bronfman family). Years later, the Mariaggi Hotel became the Marina Inn, and was unfortunately torn down in 1988—at the grand old age of 104. Captain Roland's narrative makes us nostalgic for the days when wrap-around verandahs were a part of Thunder Bay's architecture.

TLS & EAW

Life in a Thundering Bay

This location was well chosen, being on the corner of South Water and Park Streets, with an abrupt fall to the water, thereby securing one of the most essential points—good drainage. Facing a large open space of water, it commands a magnificent view of Thunder Bay, with the Cape and Welcome Islands in front, and Isle Royale in the distance. To the right is Pie Island, and further south the majestic McKay's mountain, guarding as it were the mouth of the beautiful Kaministiquia.

Where can be found a site to equal this panorama of scenery?

The architecture of the new building is modern renaissance of Queen Ann style, built with red brick. The front has large and elegantly finished verandahs to each floor, with communication with each other by means of the iron steps in cases of urgent need. The lowest verandah is continued the entire length of the building on Park Street, affording a splendid promenade. The space between the walls and woodwork has been ingeniously filled with cross pieces, and in places necessary with brick and plaster, to prevent draught in case of fire.

The main entrance is off Water Street, a dozen wide steps leading into a large and finely constructed vestibule; thence into the main lobby where one is at once struck with the beauty of both the general finish and work in detail of the interior. To the left is the writing room; on the opposite side the reading-room, facing which is the office, and in rear of that is the wash-room, finished with fine white marble, and a stairway leading to the basement into the water-closets. To the front of the basement, and immediately under the reading-room is fitted up and used as a barber shop. Under the writing

The 'Algoma' passing Thunder Cape, 1870

Where can be found a site to equal this panorama of scenery?

Advertisement for the Northern Hotel, 1887

Northern Hotel, 1887

room and on the corner is situated the cigar and tobacco store, behind which are three large and airy sample rooms for the use of commercial men. The cellar commences here and runs almost the entire length of the building. In the office a large electric bell indicator has been placed in position, connecting with every room in the house. Opposite the office is the grand stairway, wide, and built with low rises, the balustrade under the hand railing being composed of beautifully carved hard wood uprights.

On reaching the first landing an immense stained glass window, facing on Park Street, gives the surroundings a rich and elegant appearance. On gaining the first floor you turn to the right into the main drawing room and parlour, 45 × 25, with entrances to the verandah. A fine marble mantle with an open English fireplace, gives it an air of comfort. A lobby leads to the hallway of the south wing; further to the north along the lobby the hallway of the wing commences, the rooms of which are all *en suite* in two and three; this is carried on throughout the whole of the first floor. On the second floor in front the rooms are also arranged *en suite;* are large and with fine transoms with patent attachments. There are 100 bedrooms in all. A ladies' entrance with private stairway leads to every hall, and ladies' conservatories and bath-rooms are on each floor. Great attention has been given by the architect in following closely in his fine design, privacy for the lady guests, which is very requisite for a summer hotel. A delightful view is obtained from the windows in front on the top floor facing the bay.

A large water tank with a capacity of 5,000 gallons is on the top floor supplying water to the house, and connections are made with every floor, where a large amount of hose will be constantly on hand in case of fire. A back stairway in the south wing leads down to the culinary and kitchen department, the one in the north wing leading to the laundry; also two fire escapes on the outside reach from the top to the bottom of the building. The dining room is on the ground floor, 25 feet wide, and extends from the office corridor 76 feet through the south wing. The billiard room and bar occupy the same space in the north wing, with ample room for six large billiard tables, at the back end of which is the bar, with more commercial rooms in the rear. The Northern is under the direct management of Mr. F. S. Wiley, and the gentlemen in connection with this enterprise are deserving of the highest commendation, in supplying not only a long felt want, but a stern necessity, so far as first-class accommodation is concerned. Mr. R. J. Edwards was the architect.

CHAPTER FOUR

The Lost Mother Lode (1926)

By W. S. Piper

This chapter is from the book that first piqued our interest. The author, W. S. Piper, was a local hardware store owner and historian. In this story, Piper and his friend Edward, are wandering around Dog Lake with their Ojibway guide Joe, searching for the 'Lost Mother Lode' silver mine. Edward has supposedly come upon 'sure' information on where the mine is, which is 'sure' to make them millionaires. Needless to say, things do not go according to plan, and we meet the men after their escape from the Sioux Chief Blackstone[1]. The men are now on their way to meet Chief Eagle, an Ojibway chief (whose daughter, First Daughter, they had occasion to help during their travels) at the June dance. The men are hoping Chief Eagle can shed some light on where to look for the elusive mine. Piper does not tell us what year this journey takes place, but his meeting with Chief Blackstone, and the fact that he travelled by train at the start of the journey, suggests the 1880s.

TLS & EAW

W. S. Piper, c. 1925

Having had neither breakfast nor lunch we were now ravenous and as there was no prospect of a meal until we reached our camp at Dog Lake, it behoved us to get moving rapidly in that direction. The memory of that painful episode still, occasionally, disturbs my comfort. However, there was nothing to be gained by sitting down and bemoaning our hard fate so we shouldered our packs and set off down the trail with a show of energy that we were far from feeling.

After tramping for several hours we stopped to rest at a small stream where we tried to ease that painful vacuum under our belts by taking long and copious draughts of the ice cold water. It didn't help any that I could notice and Edward made matters worse by relating in detail the particulars of some very fine meals that he had eaten on a recent visit to Chicago.

The sun had kissed the Earth good-night and the dusk had merged into the gloom of darkness long before we arrived at Hotel Frozen Dog [the name of their cabin] but we were overfilled with joy at the prospect of a comfortable camp in the wilderness accompanied by a well stocked commissary department.

In less than two shakes our fire was going and Joe started to make pancakes whilst we regaled ourselves with handfuls of oatmeal and sugar. Next we removed the bacon from the rafters and, although it had grown a full set of green whiskers during our absence, we were not fastidious after our long fast, so giving it a rough shave we quickly had it sizzling in the pan.

Mercy; how we did eat. Belshazzar's feast looked like a ha'porth of fish and chips when compared with our collation. After clearing the dishes we lit our pipes, but nature's sweet restorer, sleep, soon brought to close a hard, and unusually eventful, day.

After a rather late breakfast on the following morning Joe went to visit his family, and if possible, bring us definite information on the time when Enoch Eagle might be expected to visit the settlement. We availed ourselves of this, the first free morning for a very considerable period, to take a shave, followed by a swim in the lake, and then change into a complete set of clean clothes. Refreshed in both body and mind we emerged, newly clad, from our hut exhilarated by the sparkling purity of the upland air and enthralled by the beauty of our natural surroundings enhanced by the halo of romance and mystery with which Indian legend and Indian faith had endowed it.

Joe soon returned with the good tidings that First Daughter had arrived and was ensconced as a guest with his family, being the bearer of greetings from her father who expected to arrive that same afternoon to participate in the annual festival and dance, to which we had been invited, and which was due to commence as soon as the dancing lodge was completed.

This program gave us the remainder of the day free to indulge our bent for visiting and studying the various historic points of interest in the vicinity. But first, accompanying Joe, we wended our way to the spot that was being prepared for the ceremony of the June dance.

To us, who had not been previously privileged to attend such a function, every detail of the arrangements were of great interest. The ground selected was almost perfectly level, carefully cleared and beaten down by a system of smooth, painstaking packing until it resembled a high grade hardwood floor.

Exactly in the centre stood a long pole, hewed perfectly square, finely polished and then painted with all the colours of the rainbow. This pole was the centre of a circle some fifty or sixty feet in diameter whose circumference was marked by a high fence of peeled poles painted white. At a distance it looked for all the world like a cemetery.

After spending some time at the site of this dancing lodge we proceeded about two and a half miles down the old Sioux trail to the site of one of the principal headquarters of the Sioux Nation. At this spot, on a bluff overlooking the Kaministiquia River and Little Dog Lake, was the thirty-three foot long picture of the great Sioux Ogama 'Wild Spirit Dog'[2].

Made in the form of a dog it had been excavated from the natural ground to a depth of about two feet. The mould thus prepared had then been refilled to the depth of about one foot with a white silver sand which gleamed under the hot June sun from its surrounding setting of brown or green.

This was the site of the ancient execution and torture dance and as we listened to Joe's recital of the horrible rites and ceremonies that had once desecrated this beautiful spot the poignant thought, of this, yet another illustration of man's inhumanity to man, clouded our spirits and caused a pall of gloom to descend over the spot taking all the warmth and life from the glorious sunshine. Even the light breezes that played through the pines seemed to voice the weird, wailing requiem of the helpless women and children who had suffered there.

But, following the tumultuous succession of his recital, the key note changed. The wind through the pines then told us in strong and vibrant language that the principle of eternal justice has always been, is now and ever shall be dominant on the face of the Earth. For, in their bitter hour of need Nenabushoo observed their [the Ojibway's] tribulation and called on the fiery spirit of the Great Thunder Eagle who saved them from annihilation and snatched for them a victory out of the very jaws of death [from the Sioux].

On our return to camp the afternoon was far spent so we prepared an early supper and then visited the ancient cemetery which lay by the lakeshore about a half a mile from our camp. This cemetery possessed great historic interest and had been in use for unnumbered generations. It still retained much of the quaint aspect of early days and on every side one could see evidence of the deep love lavished by these natives on the last resting place of their departed kindred. Each grave was marked by a carefully prepared and painted stake and we were particularly struck by the appearance of one small grave, evidently that of a child, which was smothered with a coverlet of beautiful wild violets. From the stake hung a little pair of beautifully worked beaded moccasins, a battered wooden doll and a dilapidated alarm clock. Pathetic tributes to the love of some devoted mother whose tears had combined with loving hands to produce the fragrant covering.

Not a single grave appeared to be neglected or forgotten. Every one was provided with some article of clothing, firearms, beads or other ornament. A spirit of deep solemnity pervaded us all and no tongue intruded on the sacred silence of that hallowed spot. We needed no Celestial reminder than we were indeed on holy ground as we slowly and silently wended our way between the graves and from there to the shore of the lake.

It was a quiet and beautiful evening, the air cool and the water smooth and inviting. We had as yet seen no canoes on the lake so, as it was reasonably certain that Enoch would appear before the departure of daylight, we watched the distant horizon as we smoked and meditated. Very soon Joe called our attention to a small black spot far to the North-East, which he assured us was a canoe, and hazarded the opinion

Life in a Thundering Bay

**On a bluff overlooking
the Kaministiquia River
and Little Dog Lake,
was the thirty-three foot long
picture of the great
Sioux Ogama Wild Spirit Dog...**

Dog Lake Effigy, no date, but sometime before 1926

that it would certainly be the canoe of Enoch Eagle as it proceeded from the direction of his dwelling place.

Shortly we were able to see for ourselves that it was a canoe and propelled by five lusty paddlers. It came up to us with great rapidity and quickly passed us, leaving a long, wide wake that shone like silver as the setting sun lit up the ripples. Joe informed us that Enoch was the striking figure in the stern and that he would proceed to the landing dock to have early converse with the visitor, reporting the result to us, at our camp, later in the evening. It was quite dark when Joe finally turned up at our camp and, in reply to our questions, informed us that Enoch had been too busy in meeting and greeting his many friends for Joe to find a suitable opportunity of having any conversation with him. He ascertained, however, that Enoch had been invited to decorate the dancing lodge with ribbons, on the morrow, and that our best plan would be to attend the ceremony with Joe and seek an opportunity for conversation.

Nothing more could be accomplished that night so Joe retired to his own place with a promise to call for us at eight o'clock the next morning. This arrangement was duly carried out and immediately after breakfast we set out to visit the dancing lodge. When the site came suddenly into view of rounding a corner we became speechless with amazement.

The place that had been so quiet and peaceful during our visit the previous evening had achieved a most extraordinary transformation. A regular forest of teepees had sprung up entirely surrounding the dancing lodge. Men, women, and children were busily moving around in every direction all intent on some business that was evidently a source of joy and satisfaction to each participant. The canoes drawn up on the beach and moored side by side at the primitive wharf formed a veritable fleet, sufficiently numerous to have transported, in the grim olden days, a mighty army of warriors.

But now no feelings of hate, revenge or strife dominated the gathering. That gala spirit of love, tolerance, and benevolence permeated the entire assembly to such a keen pitch of harmony that we felt somewhat excluded from the prevailing clan spirit as if we were strangers in a strange land and the unwitting spectators of a ceremony that we could only dimly understand and in which we were entirely incapable of participating.

At frequent intervals we caught sight of Enoch but he was always surrounded by a crowd of eager friends which discouraged us from intruding. So popular did he appear to be that we were almost in despair at the difficulty which seemed to present an impassable barrier to any conversation with him. How far, indeed, from the thoughts of this happy crowd, appeared our mundane thoughts obsessed by the quest for wealth from nature's store-house.

As we walked several times around the lodges, not a single individual spoke to us and the numerous glances directed at us, some curious and many frankly suspicious, added little to our peace of mind. It seemed useless to spend any more time in waiting around. Amidst these surroundings Enoch appeared to be more unapproachable than a king on his throne, so with depressed and dampened spirits we turned our backs on this scene of gaiety in which we had no part and adjourned to the shore of the lake.

Here we sat and watched the natives drawing and setting their fishing nets in, probably, the identical manner of their forefathers of hundreds of years ago.

There seemed to be no alternative but to pack our duffle and abandon our expedition, but Joe vigorously opposed this

**A spirit of deep solemnity
pervaded us all and no
tongue intruded on the
sacred silence
of that hallowed spot . . .**

Ojibway graves in Northern Ontario, 1857

alternative. He assured us that if we only would wait until the dance started that we would have many opportunities of speaking with Enoch. Further that as he was aware of our desire to speak with him that he would be displeased at our departure when, it was obvious, that he was engaged in the, to him, very important preliminaries leading up to this sacred ceremony.

So, after wandering aimlessly through many of the woodland paths, we again returned to the dancing lodge and seated ourselves on a log near the entrance, from which point of vantage we watched this seemingly irresponsible crowd of merry makers enjoy themselves. At the same time feeling in our inmost souls that the Divine Fates had pre-ordained for us the earning of our daily bread by the sweat of our brows instead of by the more easy method that we had had the temerity to desire.

Great Falls on the Little Dog River, 1857

After sitting there for some time we saw three women approach us and as they drew nearer the leader hastened towards us with outstretched hand and a friendly smile, greeting us in perfectly clear English with the words, "Welcome to Dog Lake". This was First Daughter, accompanied by Joe's wife and her daughter. That we were surprised is to state the case mildly. Edward's eyes stood out like the stops on an organ and the power of speech had entirely departed from me. This happy looking, self possessed girl in the midst of her own people was an entirely different creature from the shy, native girl whom we had so recently befriended and whose remarks had been entirely confined to sentences in her mother tongue.

"I hope you are having a good time here," she said, "and I want you to come and meet my Father."

Ye gods; this was the one thing that we really wanted at that time, so gathering our scattered wits together, we assured her that we would be more than delighted to make his acquaintance.

"Come with me," she commanded, and we promptly set out in her wake, threading our way amongst innumerable groups of people, for all of whom she had a smile or a cheerful word, until we entered the dancing lodge where Enoch was the centre of an inevitable group. Catching him unceremoniously by the coat she pulled him around to face in our direction and said something to him in her native tongue. At this he looked towards us with a friendly smile and approached us.

"Father," introduced First Daughter, "these are the good men who were so kind to me."

This, the most flattering introduction possible placed us under great obligation to First Daughter and, as she was shortly to be married, it was essential that we reciprocate to the extent of a wedding present.

Now that we had met Enoch we no longer had the slightest doubt as to the sincerity and depth of our welcome. First Daughter was evidently the pride of her Father's heart and his welcome was so spontaneous that we felt that he literally radiated friendship and good-will, to which he added every form of courtesy and thoughtfulness so that the feeling of strangeness departed from us and we knew that we were welcome visitors.

Enoch was an educated man of considerable polish with striking and handsome features and, although a pure bred Ojibway, he spoke English and French with great fluency. As a fur trader he had been in the employ of one of the great fur Companies for many years and had established an unassailable reputation for honesty and integrity. His large, soft and velvety eyes gleamed with pleasure as he bade us welcome and invited us to stay for the dance.

We assured him that nothing would give us greater pleasure than to witness the calumet dance [the calumet is a ceremonial pipe] of which we had heard so much.

"Then you must stay," he concluded. "We always celebrate the smoke dance on this spot. It is one of the most sacred of the Ojibway dances for this pipe of peace is the symbol of our great annual sacrament to the Manitou."

After a few minutes of general conversation we broached the subject that lay so closely to our thoughts, and asked him if we could engage him as a guide to assist us in our exploration and search for the Lost Mother Mine, and before parting with him that day we had secured his consent to act in that capacity on an expedition for which we would make the necessary arrangements for the coming Autumn. He assured us, however, that it was most unlikely that the mine was on this side of the lake. He had trapped and traded around Dog Lake for over twenty years and that, if such a mine existed in that territory, he would most certainly have heard of it.

"From what you say and from other scraps of information that I have heard, I am convinced that the mine is closer to Lake Superior and that a boat will be essential if you are to continue your search with any prospect of success. However, we will go carefully into the details of the matter on some future occasion," said Enoch, as he returned to his duties in connection with the dance.

This conclusion very effectually dampened our recently revived hopes as we had not previously had any doubts that we would return triumphantly from our present trip, the proud owners of the greatest mine in all history. However, matters would have to remain in abeyance until after the dance and so, pre-occupied with our varied thoughts, we returned to camp.

When the broad, panoramic vista of Dog Lake first unfolded itself before our admiring eyes, with its green tree studded islands set in their sapphire bed stretching as far as the eye could see, we were convinced that Nature could have chosen no fitter setting for the location of one of her richest treasure houses.

Added to the aesthetic beauty of the scene we saw at the same time abundant water powers in many cascading falls combined with a wealth of timber trees as practically useful as they were beautiful; both essential features in the economical and profitable exploration of a modern silver mine, and probably no one will criticize this rather utilitarian thought in the presence of such wonderful beauty.

Among the many tumultuous thoughts that crowded our minds we could not help thinking how strange it was that after

Life in a Thundering Bay

Chief Skeet presenting the calumet to the Great Spirit, c. 1925

a full month of exploration, involving every sort of physical hardship in packing, climbing and staking claims in wet and cold and heat, that we appeared to be as far away as ever from the discovery of the Mother Mine of our dreams that constantly occupied our every waking thought and most of our visions of sleep.

Up to this time we had been guided by others as to the likeliest places in which to find such mineral to the exclusion of any personal ideas we had on the subject but we had, by this time, acquired enough experience to reach some very important conclusions. First we concluded that, in the mining business, the most beautiful scenery and the most definite holes in the ground do not invariably produce a silver mine.

Further, that visions and dreams unharnessed to experience led us to no practical achievements. In addition we were getting very firmly convinced that Joe did not know where the Lost Mother Mine was or, if he did, he would not show it to us.

About ten o'clock that night we left our camp to stroll through the bush contiguous to the lake and watched the lights die out, one by one, from island after island across the lake, many of which were occupied as summer homes by Indians of the Dog Lake Band. Near midnight the darkness was complete and the whole earth seemed to slumber in calm repose in an atmosphere that was at once placid, silent and still, yet, withal, charged, electrical, ghostly and, in a sense, ominous. Shortly, the heavens began to awaken and the goddess of the Northern Lights proceeded to hold her revels across the firmament, flashing and dancing from every point of the compass towards the Zenith in every variation of shape and form in lambent hues of pale amber, rose and blood red.

The stars shone with a fitful, restless brilliance and the whole atmosphere was wild, strange and exciting, more like the imagination of a fevered dream than the cold, hard reality of a Northern light.

Suddenly, from the North appeared a green ball of fire with a velocity and curvature as though it had been a distress rocket fired from the deck of a disabled vessel. It appeared to come directly towards us, followed by streamers of brilliantly coloured sparks, then arching overhead it disappeared on the horizon where Thunder Cape stood sentinel, dark, and silent on the sombre night bosom of Lake Superior beyond the deep forest that encircled us.

Almost immediately a glorious flood of light appeared at the summit of the arch of heaven and poured its perpendicular rays in a stupendous flood upon the silent world below, dimming the starry hosts until they faded into twinkling pin-points as though removed to further vast distances from those they occupy.

Soon this brilliant light concentrated and assumed the form of a gigantic bird with luminous, outstretched wings; the whole sparkling bright with a sheen of richer satin than mortal ever devised. For several minutes the glorious heavenly vision hovered almost directly over us and then majestically glided after the setting sun and disappeared over the Western horizon.

After some minutes of deep silence Edward remarked: "I wonder if we were the only ones to be privileged to see that vision? The islands are in darkness and I think it unlikely that any of the Dog Lake Band were awake to see it. I am glad that it looked at us for I verily believe it was an angel."

Then, for a time, we felt that we were in another World, but were soon aroused from a delicious reverie by the haunting melody of a strangely weird and mournful song whose cadence called as from someone in distress.

Cautiously we moved in the direction from which the sound appeared to come and were astonished to see, within a short distance, the reflection of a fire. Approaching the fire we discovered an Indian engaged in repairing a drum whilst squatting on the ground. To our courteous enquiry as to what was going on that night he made no reply. As if he had neither heard nor seen us he arose to his feet and walked silently and quickly away. At a distance of a few rods we followed him until we came to a small fire that had been made in the centre of a considerable clearing and around which were seated several Indians, all of whom were smoking. By the light of the fire we were able to identify Enoch Eagle with a particularly large pipe in his hand and promptly asked him to explain to us what they were doing.

"We are making a medicine to the Great Spirit," he at once replied and then proceeded to make us welcome with a grave

Beginning of the Great Dog Portage on Dog Lake, 1857

and dignified courtesy that impressed us deeply and he extended an invitation to us to stay for the service about to be held.

For our benefit, he explained in a few words of English that the phenomenon that we had just been privileged to witness was the manifestation of the great 'Fiery Eagle of Thunder Cape', an emissary of the first rank in the service of Nenabushoo.

The service consisted largely of singing interspersed with the ceremonial smoking of Kinikinic. The mixture prepared from the inside bark of the red willow to which is added certain quantities of Virginia tobacco and Burberry leaves. The red willow, having been stained with the blood of Nenabushoo is sacred to the Manitou. The blood of sacrifice that has come down through the ages by way of Abraham's ram, the lamb of the Jewish Passover and even that of the Holy Eucharist is visualized for the Indian in the blood red pigment of the red willow. From its slender branches are fashioned the stems of all their ceremonial pipes and the tender inside bark is the basis of the mixture smoked therein. Its pungent fumes are, to them, a holy incense that ascends as an acceptable peace offering even unto the throne of God. To them, this ceremony is nothing less than the most holy sacrament and to refuse to smoke from the pipe thus offered is, not only the greatest insult that can be given an Indian, but is sacrilege almost beyond pale. Only by humbly confessing your unworthiness to participate can you hope for any possibility of forgiveness.

The solemnity of the scene, combined with the faith and grandeur of the idea filled me with awe and affected me deeply as I realized that in this far distant place, although in a different form, I was face to face with the essentials of the old Egyptian faith that for countless centuries guided the souls of mankind.

Later, I ascertained that the responsibility for the Flood was ascribed, in Indian legend, to the red willow. It was revealed that Nenabushoo, being desirous that the red willow should be widely disseminated throughout the whole World so that it would be readily available for the use and comfort of all her children, collected a large quantity of seed. This seed she stained and fertilized with her life blood and then proceeded to scatter it from every mountain top so that it drifted down the slopes and found a resting place throughout all the valleys and plains beneath, where it thrived mightily close to the teepees of her children, there, the flaming red willow, changing in colour from bright to sombre as sunshine and shadow passed, furnished abundant material for the accepted sacrifice, enabling them to make perpetually a peace offering to God and, through the pipe, hold communion with the

Manitou, the Great Controlling Creative Spirit of their Mythology.

Soon after the plan of Nenabushoo had been fulfilled and the glory of the red willow had spread itself all over the Earth, the Great Serpent observed the glow of this wonderful colouring covering the entire Earth and its war-like challenge provoked him to great wrath. He immediately made plans to set out with the intention of utterly destroying the red willow which he sensed to be antagonistic to his evil domination over the minds and souls of mankind. Nenabushoo, ever watchful for her works and welfare of her children, immediately defied him to attempt the destruction of her beautiful handicraft and soon fierce fight was raging. It was not long before Nenabushoo pierced the spiritual heart of the Great Serpent with a fiery arrow which caused him to break off the fight and hurry to the Ocean where, in his distress, he blew his venom into the water and so poisoned it that it remains undrinkable to the present day. Then Nenabushoo, realizing what he had done, decided that the whole Earth must be purged from this pollution. So she then proceeded to the top of the highest mountain and there pulled on the fiery rope that ascends into the heavens; and the heavens opened and the floods descended so that the waters of heaven covered the whole face of the Earth and the Earth remained beneath the Flood many days.

The next morning broke clear and hot with an unnaturally brilliant light that caused the distant hills to stand out clearly as if they had moved more closely to our encampment. This, we knew, presaged a storm and soon heavy banks of cumulus and nimbus clouds began rolling up from the Western horizon. As we had had over four weeks of unseasonably dry weather it was evident to us that we were in for a prolonged and heavy spell of rain that would postpone the dance for at least two or three days. Consequently, we sent Joe to invite Enoch to visit our camp for dinner. They soon returned together, Enoch being very depressed at the gloomy prospects for the dance. We feigned deep regret at the untoward interruption of a ceremony that we were so anxious to see, but in our inward hearts we were secretly delighted at the intervention of the rain because it afforded us the opportunity of questioning Enoch at great length.

The storm broke with great fury accompanied by heavy squalls of hail whose terrific stones, as large as hen's eggs, glistened and danced as they rebounded from the ground. Where they fell in the bush they wrought havoc with the leaves and limbs of the trees and spread the petals of the wild flowers in all directions.

Soon the wind fell to a soft steady breeze, the canopy of cloud assumed a dull, even, leaded hue and the rain fell with a steady, tenacious persistence that lasted for a full two days and nights. We persuaded Enoch to make his home at our camp during the remainder of our visit to Dog Lake and, in the warmth of the fire, he laid aside his disappointment and beguiled us with many interesting stories of the land and its inhabitants, his reminiscences reaching back hundreds of years into the dim and distant past, long before the foot of a white man had trodden the North Shore of Lake Superior.

Included amongst them was the history of Ogama, Wild Spirit Dog and Green Mantle as well as a masterly exposition of the Indian religious beliefs. As we questioned him regarding his faith in Kitchie Manitou and Nenabushoo and listened to his deeply sincere and picturesque enunciation of his abiding faith we felt that we were, indeed, sitting at the feet of Gamaliel . . . .

It is proper that I should place on record some of these old stories as they have been related to me so often that they have almost become part of my own outlook. There are two Deities in the Indian religion; Manitou, the Supreme God, and Nenabushoo. There is also the evil spirit, Matchie Manitou. Consequently, I asked Enoch to describe for us the attributes of these characters. To this request he replied:—

"Kitchie Manitou (God) is the Great Spirit to whom all our prayers are offered, the one Supreme Being in whose keeping lies the destiny of the whole Universe. His voice speaks to us in the wind, in the thunder, in the great storms, in the waters, and in the forest through the trees. Everywhere he speaks to us that we may not lie, steal, hate, or unnecessarily destroy the works of Nenabushoo, but rather obey and hearken to her voice. Then there is Nenabushoo, owner of the Earth, of the same age as the Earth, her food is 'time' and she cannot grow old because she continually renews herself. We are permitted to call her 'Friend', but she is much more that our friend, she is our Mother. Her home is with the Manitou and the spirits of our dead.

"When the Earth is wrapped in sorrow and gloom she sends her watch lights trailing down the sky, surrounding the Earth with great shafts of fire that all men may see, and take warning lest the Great Thunder Eagle, in all its glorious colours, should appear in majesty over Thunder Cape. For this is our Covenant that tells us the Manitou has not forgotten us. She is patient and long suffering, slow to wrath, loving, and kind, but those who continually disobey her laws she wallops without mercy.

"Lastly there is the Evil One, Matchie Manitou, known as the smooth, slick robber, the liar and enemy of all mankind who wages relentless war on all the higher aspirations of the human race. He is endowed with innumerable disguises, is able to take any shape or impersonate any character and has the power to call any number of other beings to his assistance, who are submerged in evil even as he is submerged. Under the protection of his various disguises he is able to accomplish such a record of crime, deceit and deviltry that it is impossible for the mind of simple man to even partially comprehend it. His first appearance on Earth was in the form of a copper coloured serpent, our copper head snake, the most treacherous, vindictive and poisonous of all reptiles."

As he finished speaking both awe and wonder filled our hearts at the poetic beauty of his conception of the main springs of eternal life, so impressively supported by that simple and sincere faith that one could readily believe possessed the power to remove mountains or perform miracles. And so, for the two days and much of the nights, we conversed with our distinguished guest on subjects both grave and gay, not forgetting every possible reference to any point that might shed light on the location of the Lost Mother Mine. This visit was of more than passing interest to us for it was on this spot that we were admitted, for all time, into the intimate friendship of the Indians by means of the solemn ceremony of the sacred calumet.

Henceforth we were free to attend any of their ceremonials, whether tribal or religious, and this admittance to their friendship could only be regarded in the light of a great honour and a most sacred privilege. This point of view was most indelibly impressed on us a few days later with stupendous force when the soul stirring passages of the Christening prayer had been translated into English for our benefit. Their clear definite belief in the immortality of the soul, a wide and all-embracing spiritual life of which their own individual spirits formed an inseparable and definite part and intuitively formed and completed the beautiful structure of their belief which was tenaciously and completely held to be the foundation and controlling essence of their being, their stay and guide throughout life, here and hereafter.

The completeness of their belief in dreams was difficult for us to understand for no matter of importance would ever be undertaken or decided until guidance had been sought by means of a dream. When the Medicine Man consults his dream he always wears the Kinin [see description on pg. 84] over his heart for it is the light of his dream and in its radiance only may he be guided to a clear and proper interpretation of the message that his dream conveys.

On being advised of the potency of dream communication we asked if their dreams ever demanded the sacrifice of a human life. We were told that such had been the case on rare occasions and related a case in which such a sacrifice had been demanded.

Our informant: "Many years ago when we were at war with our ancient enemies, the Sioux, a head man of the village of Flint Lake dreamt that unless a human sacrifice was offered up that every member of the tribe would be put to death. He quickly assembled all the inhabitants of the village and announced that he had had a dream that he feared was beyond his power to carry out. His dream demanded a human sacrifice, a young woman and his own daughter was named as the appropriate victim. She was to be put to death by his own hand at sunset so that her soul might accompany the sun beyond the stars. Her flesh was to be burned and her bones buried in the bosom of the Earth.

"This announcement deeply agitated the tribe but its message was immediately accepted for none dared doubt its supreme authority. Preparations for the sacrifice were put in hand at once, a site chosen for the ceremony and its accompanying feast and lavish decoration of brilliantly coloured draping contrasted vividly with the sombre green of the forest glade. The girl was then beautifully attired in a rich ceremonial dress of an Indian Princess and led to the place of execution by her own girlfriends where they found the entire population assembled all eager to make the remaining hours of life pleasant to the innocent and unsuspecting victim whose soul was to pass out and on as the declining sun sought its nightly haven beyond the Western hills. Just as the lower rim touched the encircling horizon the maiden was led, with all honour, to the place of execution.

"It was only then, as one by one the whole tribe approached her, touched her, and turned with tears away, that she realized that she was to be offered as a sacrifice.

"With realization came action; tearing the flowers from her hair she called loudly to God for Him to save her from this bitter fate and as her father stepped into the circle, with stabbing spear in hand, the cries of the girl, conjoined with the sobs and prayers of the people, were heart-rending. Her father, with uplifted hands, implored the people to be silent and then explained to them that his dream demanded his child and that all good men must be loyal to their dreams. As for his daughter, for her to die at that time assured her immediate entry to everlasting happiness and the saving of the tribe from most terrible ill-fortune. As he finished speaking his daughter threw herself on the ground and cried aloud:

'My father, don't give me to death, don't give me to death, that terrible beast.'

"Not to be deterred from his purpose he raised his spear in striking attitude and a deep shudder ran through the crowd as all thought that the death blow was descending. But even as his arm tensed for that terrible blow his face changed and the spear fell from his hand as he shrieked in a loud voice, 'My dream is satisfied.' He then lighted his calumet and pointed it to the heavens, singing and glorifying God. Then was a great feast prepared and with music and dancing the thanksgiving of the tribe was offered to the Deity throughout the night.

"Every detail of this event was quickly reported to the headquarters of the Sioux on Dog Mountain for the Sioux had many signal stations and were skilled beyond all other North American tribes in the art and practice of signalling. All the tribes looked on signalling as a matter of the greatest importance and the Ojibway station on Thunder Mountain used over 600 signs and their allies, the Cree, had developed the method of signalling known as 'Tuning the Waters' to an uncanny pitch of perfection."

We further learned from our informant that Flint Village was one of the wealthiest on the whole North Shore of Lake Superior for it was the headquarters of the principle ammunition works of the great Ojibway nation.

At this point they made cutlery, spears, and arrowheads as well as furnishing the raw material, in the form of flint flakes, that were converted into spear and arrow points when shipped to the numerous other armouries of that Nation. In addition, these flakes were used universally amongst the tribes as a medium of exchange, adding materially to the prosperity of this community. Very shortly after the happy ending of the dream ceremonial of sacrifice the Ojibway spies reported active preparations for war being made in the chief encampment of the Sioux at Dog Mountain and many spies of

Ogama Dog, their notorious and vindictive leader, were captured close to the vicinity of Flint Village.

Action by the Ojibway became imperative and an army of picked men was promptly dispatched from Thunder Mountain under the command of Bukwujenene Dahyhe Owk Metigwahke (Wild man of the Forest), a great War Chief and General of the Ojibway, his sobriquet was the 'Wall-Eyed General'. He was a man of great stature and, in battle, his face was always painted a brilliant red with circles of white surrounding his eyes. To this was added a feathered war head dress, tipped with red, giving him a most blood thirsty appearance combined with dignity and strength, marking him as a great warrior, a worthy leader of the armies of his people.

Immediately on his arrival at Flint Village he called a Council of War at which it was decided to fortify the village by erecting a barricade of rocks and timber encircling the whole encampment and so provided a sheltered wall behind which the defence could be conducted. Scarcely had the defences been completed when they were vigorously attacked by overwhelming forces that soon topped the wall at many points where the Sioux judged the defence to be weakest and there concentrated their attack. Wild Man skillfully handled his forces and rushed strong parties of his reserves whenever a break occurred, but numbers were out-weighing him and the situation was nothing short of desperate. From his wigwam the Medicine Man quietly observed the tide of battle as it ebbed and flowed until a stage was reached when he deemed that action was necessary.

Quietly he lit his calumet and pointed it towards the heavens whilst chanting a supplication to God, moving from time to time to the fiercest points of attack and counter attack. Soon the sky darkened and one could see on distant Thunder

Cape the flaming pinions of the Thunder Eagle reaching the Zenith in great shafts of flame which quickly drove stupendous masses of nimbus clouds directly to Flint Village. As they approached they gathered speed, finally breaking with the terrific fury of primeval and elemental force with the concentrated thunders of all ages rolled into one awful person of continuous sound illuminated by a ceaseless flashing of the most intense lightning. Then came the rain. The heavens opened and discharged a deluge of cold, numbing, electrically charged ice-water. The heart of the Sioux failed them for fear; those without the wall threw down their arms and fled wildly to escape annihilation. Within the wall, the entire enemy were quickly slaughtered.

The heavenly manifestation that had brought terror and panic to the Sioux brought only strength, hope, and renewed courage to the Ojibway. From that day forward no enemy has dared attempt an attack on the Flint Village (Peewahnug Sahguhegun), stronghold of the Ojibway Nation . . . .

River of Life

When he had finished speaking I asked him why it was that when the Indians take their offerings to Thunder Cape that they place them only at the Lion's Head and never at the Giant's Head or the Eagle's nest and whether the other sacred beasts were held in the same veneration. Without answering this question he arose saying: "I will be back soon."

Enoch then went to his own camp and after a short time we could see him returning carrying a flat box about two feet long shaped like a suit case. Coming in he placed the box at his feet and sat down without any reference to my question or telling us what the box contained. This was certainly challenging our

Soon the sky darkened and one could see on distant Thunder Cape the flaming pinions of the Thunder Eagle

Sioux Dress and Moccasions, 1860

curiosity but we knew that it would not further our purpose if we appeared to be too anxious. We were, however, getting restless when he finally arose and took off his hat, coat, and vest, then proceeded, with a look of great reverence to open the box. The first article he took out was a pipe with a stem about two feet in length and a large red stone head. Next came a beautifully decorated beadwork medicine bag from which he took an ornamental pouch which he called his Kini-Kinic bag. Then he lifted out his gown which was covered with the most wonderful beadwork I had ever seen which he told us weighed 35 lbs. It was beautiful beyond words to describe and was literally gorgeous, its main features being a perfectly worked eagle that covered the whole chest. This gown, together with his feathered head dress, he handed to us to inspect and admire and secured our unstinted praise of this beautiful work done by the hands of these skilled needle-workers.

Enoch then donned this costume and, as we looked at him, we felt that we were in the presence of a great Indian priest. He then let us see the ceremonial stone, 'Artiface', and stated that anyone possessing one of these rare stones was favoured by the Great Spirit, Manitou, and was highly respected by man; also that if the possessor had an enemy, that enemy will die before the possessor. The last article he produced greatly aroused our curiosity and he called it 'Kinin'.

On examination we found it to consist of three pieces, each about two and a half inches long and five-eights of an inch in diameter. One piece was of copper, one of stone and one was made from the large bone of the wing of an owl. All were perfectly round, highly polished and pierced by a hole through the centre. They were hung on a wine coloured cord through which ran a thread of gold. These three elements, he explained to us, represented three different spirits; the spirit of the copper, the spirit of the stone and the spirit of the owl, which gave light to his dream when worn over his heart; the dream resembles the firefly and can only be seen by the light of its Kinin. He then filled and lighted his calumet and soon our camp was full of the aroma of the incense from its bowl. Not until then did he mention the question that we had asked of him. Without preface, he began: "The figure on Thunder Cape, which you mentioned, that watches the sun go down, is one of the sacred and mighty beasts, it is Nenabushoo's Heraldid Lion and is the symbol of Death. All life must pass this lion before it can enter the Happy Hunting Ground. Where is the Happy Hunting Ground? No living man knows just where it is and we of this World must be satisfied to serve the Great Spirit. I have seen it in a Vision but I have never been there, if I had, I could not have returned. My vision came from my dream."

Nipigon River, looking south from High Rock Portage, 1870

"Have you known anyone else to have a Vision?" we asked.

"Yes," he replied, "Perhaps four or five, I am not sure. There are three stages to this Happy Hunting Ground. The first is the worldly stage, the second is the Death Stage and the last is the River of Life. I must tell you that my ambition as a young man was to become a great Medicine Man. I attended every medicine dance to which I was invited. I have, also, prayed and fasted for ten days on the Nipigon Dream Stone and came through without mishap, although many others failed and had to be taken off because they were unable to stand the long fast and exposure of the ordeal. My father sailed a boat for one of the Fur Trading Companies, gathering furs from the trading posts of Lake Superior, often voyaging as far as Sault Saint Marie. One Fall my father went down the shore for a cargo of salt fish that had been caught and salted by the Indians for the Company's trading posts.

"The season was getting late and, day by day, we walked the shore anxiously watching for any sign of his boat. One day our hearts were gladdened by the sight of a signal fire on Welcome Islands, the usual notification that a boat was in sight. We eagerly watched, and at sundown we sighted a boat abreast of the Welcomes apparently heading strongly for the mouth of the Mission River. The wind had increased in strength and it was blowing hard from the North-East with occasional flurries of snow. As darkness fell the gale increased to a heavy storm with blinding snow. We watched all through that never to be forgotten night and at daybreak we anxiously scanned the still heaving waters of the Lake. The storm had passed and peace reigned beneath a smiling sky, but no speck of sail or sign of boat could be seen on all the vast expanse of waters. Many hours later some wreckage was washed ashore on the sands near the mouth of the Mission River which remains there to the present day. The sight of this wreck completely upset my Mother and for many days she, with others, ceaselessly walked the shore as they watched the Lake for some sign of my father for the wreck was not that of my father's boat, it having come from the South Shore.

"For my part I decided to locate my father by means of my dream; so, taking a few things to afford me warmth, I set up my teepee on the first ledge of Thunder Mountain in a position where, sheltered from the North-West wind, I commanded a wide view of the Lake and surrounding country. I then commenced to fast and pray whilst making a medicine to the Great Spirit. On the fourth day my teepee began to sway backwards and forwards and I knew that I was in communication with the Dead.

"My fire died out but I felt neither cold nor hunger; the sound of sweetest music filled the air and I was in another World. I had arrived at a landing stage apparently composed of smooth solid rock. In every direction people were eagerly hurrying as though anxiously seeking something so I followed the crowd. I had not proceeded far until I heard my guardian spirit speak to me some kindly words of welcome, so I followed my spirit to what appeared to be the entrance to a beautiful avenue of trees where I was startled to see an immense beast made from the strongest metals which, as it stretched its enormous joints, seemed to crack with every movement, and I stopped instantly.

"'Be not afraid,' my guardian spirit said. 'That is the sacred lion, the symbol of Death, guarding the entrance to the River of Life. If you pass that Great Beast you cannot return to the Earth, for that is the Rule in this Land of Death. You are greatly privileged to see these marvellous sights and be allowed to again return to Earth and tell your people. Suppose we seek a place where we can get a better view and talk more freely apart from this crowd,' suggested my guardian spirit.

"Proceeding to the right bank of the River of Life a most glorious sight lay before us. Thousands of people were gathered at the foot of the steps leading up to the sacred lion, each intent on his own worship, waiting to enter the River of Life, and at intervals paeons of the most wonderful music enveloped us. Presently, it seemed as if a great gate had swung silently open and we were permitted to view the glorious vision of the other World. The River of Life took on the form of a stream of moving lights; the spirits of the Dead moving like the pulsating rhythm of the heart, lights large and small, some the merest specks which my guardian spirit explained were the spirits of little children.

"At the entrance to the celestial land there was an immense crowd seemingly welcoming some important spirit and there I beheld and recognized my father who raised his hand to silently salute me, his face radiant with joy. Turning, he laid his hand on the head of the most beautiful girl I had ever seen, and a voice came out to me that said, 'Green Mantle'. Then I awoke, knowing that my father had gone to the Happy Hunting Ground. This was the vision that my Dream saw."

Later we heard more of the great Ojibway Legend that speaks of the River of Life.

Nenabushoo (Nature)

In particular, we heard with the deepest interest Enoch's recital of the share that Nenabushoo had taken in keeping open the approaches through which humanity can only gain access to, and embark on, the Divine River. His interpretation of this incident of the Legend was again most impressively given. He said:

"By many people, who know little or nothing of our Indian beliefs, Nenabushoo is always depicted as a very mysterious being or spirit when they try to produce an Indian story, and even many of our own people tell the most ridiculous tales about this great Spirit which is known in the English language as 'Nature'.

"Some like to think of Nature as an old, old man with a hump on his back, with long white hair and a long white flowing beard, sitting on the rim of the Northern World and stirring up the Northern Lights with a stick in order that he may keep himself warm. Nothing could be further from the truth than such a description of Nenabushoo, for she is the emblem of 'Love', young and divinely fair, endowed with the gift of eternal youth and is one of the greatest of the 'Daughters of Heaven' but, even so, she is not all-powerful. Many people blame her for all their troubles but they forget that there is another spirit of tremendous power who wages constant warfare against Nature and her Government.

"This spirit is Matchie Manitou (The Devil), an evil god having vast power over the lives of men. He can turn himself into the form of a man and can also take possession of men's hearts, causing them to hate and destroy one another. Nature, on the other hand contends that she is entitled to the life that she has created and claims jurisdiction over the spirit in order that she may guide it in safety to her spiritual home, just as a mother would wish to do for her child, for the faithful children of Nenabushoo are heirs to this land. They are received there by their ministering spirits, but these spirits are not servants, they are companions of the children and the children of Nature are all regarded as gods.

"Nature has fought many fierce battles for her children and the first, and fiercest fight between these two great powers took place at the entrance to the River of Life. Matchie Manitou, having taken the form of a huge serpent with a human head crowned by two large balls of hair done up on his forehead, stretched his body across the entrance to the River of Life.

"Before its portals awaited many who were entitled to enter but there was no possible way of passing this sinister and loathsome obstacle and the spirits of these people were filled with despair. In front of them stretched the great enemy of mankind and behind them loomed the figure of Death. So, apparently, there was nothing that they could do but to return to their dead bodies on Earth in the hope that some of their friends had placed food on their graves to sustain them until they were allowed to enter the Promised Land.

"But Love is the mainspring of Life and even then the Spirit of Love was hastening to the rescue of her children. Soon, they were startled by the terrific booming of thunder, like unto the beating of thousands of mighty drums, and presently, in the midst of a blinding flash of lightning, appeared the spirit of Nature radiating her love for them and her sympathy in their distress.

"Throwing off her royal mantle she immediately started to fight the great serpent, rapidly shooting her fiery arrows at his loathsome body. All these he deftly caught and venomously threw them back at her, inflicting grievous wounds and causing her great pain. But when she was most sorely stressed a voice from Heaven spoke clearly as a silver trumpet, saying, 'Shoot him in the hair.'

"Changing her aim, she very soon succeeded in clipping the two balls of hair from his forehead and thus put him entirely out of action. This closed the fight but the vast, inert body of the serpent still closed the portals of the entrance to the River of Life. Suddenly from Heaven, heralded by a piercing scream, appeared a Great Fiery Eagle that swooped down on Matchie Manitou and buried his talons deep in the serpentine body. Rising majestically with his burden he quickly relieved himself of the weight by casting it into the air through which it fell to Earth, and has so remained here to the present day. Thus was the entry to the River of Life opened for all time for the passage of the children of Nenabushoo.

"These two are the great powers and they are like unto great governments; the one with the greatest number of warriors prevails and so holds the supreme power. We Indians are very religious, we do not take God's name in vain and there are no profane words contained in our language, but we make presents to the wonderful forms created by Nature, calling them the children of Nenabushoo. We have also vigorously waged war against the Evil One in the persons of those who have turned themselves over to him, such as witches and Windigos" . . . .

Just before retiring at the close of the second day we inspected the heavens which seemed to be getting rapidly exhausted of their moisture. Enoch confidently predicted that the rain was practically over and that a gloriously fine tomorrow would see the inauguration of the dance.

Early the next morning, in such weather as he had predicted, Enoch left Joe for the dancing lodge but Edward and I then promptly forgot all about the impending ceremony and fell to discussing every little scrap of information that had fallen from the lips of Enoch that might have even the remotest bearing on the Lost Mother Mine. We were abruptly disturbed by the unceremonious entry of a young Indian.

Carrying a small pipe in his hand he proceeded to the stove and lifted a small red ember which he placed in the bowl.

He then handed the pipe to Edward, saying, "I carry the pipe from Joe Turtle and Enoch Eagle to you men and you are required to attend the dance of the Dog Lake Band of the Ojibway."

We each solemnly took a few puffs from the beautifully ornate pipe which ceremony, we had previously ascertained from Joe, constituted an acceptance of the invitation. The pipe itself was a work of art and well worthy of description. It was about twenty inches long made of a beautiful polished red rock which we knew to be the famous Nipigon Red Rock. The hardwood stem was elaborately decorated with coloured bead work, ribbon and fur. The tobacco had been skillfully blended with herbs producing a delightful aroma.

The great day had at length arrived and we hurried through our mid-day meal to be early at the dancing lodge where a most gorgeous, and never to be forgotten scene met our eyes. Countless people were moving around in gala dress, many of the women wearing shawls of the most gorgeous hues, and some of them painted in brilliant colours. We rather timidly advanced to join the throng, but were met by welcoming smiles on every side, several people moving aside to make room for us between our friends Joe and Enoch.

Soon the orchestra, which consisted of ten drummers on the large drums and three on the small drums, took their places around the centre pole. The process of tuning was accompanied by a good deal of noise as one by

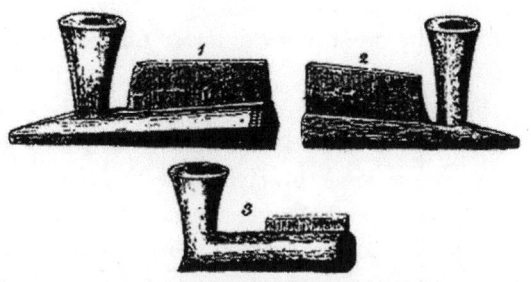

Tobacco Pipes of the Ojibways of Rainy Lake, &c.

I carry the pipe from Joe Turtle and Enoch Eagle to you men and you are required to attend the dance of the Dog Lake Band of the Ojibway.

one they placed the faces of the drums over the heat of the fire, tapping softly until the sound indicated that the correct tension had been achieved.

It was almost three o'clock before the actual ceremony, the dedication of the calumet, took place but time passed quickly as Joe and Enoch explained to us the properties of each of the drum heads, all of which were made of the skins of either animals or fish, the finest toned drums of them all being made from the skin of the sturgeon. The calumet dance is invariably given by those who have been privileged to either make or decorate the calumet, or by someone who has been presented with the calumet for some conspicuous deed of bravery.

The drums having been all tuned to the apparent satisfaction of the musicians the leader raised his drum to his ear and began to play and sing in soft tones, one by one the remainder of the orchestra chimed in until the whole air seemed filled with the perfect harmony of the weird and fascinating music.

The music stopped as the dancers, preceded by their leader, entered the ring, all painted and clothed in elaborately beaded costumes. In the left hand of the leader was held the calumet. He was easily the most striking personage in the vast assembly, his coat being worked with beads into an elaborate design, helped by a highly decorated apron. His leggings were a work of art carried out in beads and bells finished off by moccasins embellished with the many coloured quills of the porcupine. But conspicuous above all was his head dress of eagle's feathers held around his forehead by a heavily beaded band from which were suspended beaded pendants which covered his ears.

Approaching the fire he dropped to his knees and placed a live ember in the bowl of his pipe. Arising to his feet he then, with radiant face and an attitude of more than mortal ecstasy, held the pipe high above his head as an offering to the Manitou. Then bending low he touched the ground with the pipe, an offering to the Earth. Then, in rotation, pointing the pipe to the four cardinal points of heaven, the North, the East, the South, and the West, he passed it around to those within the lodge.

At this moment, the drums, whistles, rattles, and singers broke into full chorus and the dance began. The striking leader, although an elderly man, stepped with an ease and natural grace that is attained by few. The dancers followed, imitating his steps as closely as possible. Occasionally he would point the pipe at one of the onlookers who would gravely bow in acknowledgement. After the dance had proceeded for some time the shrill sound of the whistle brought it to a temporary close and we were now invited to the feast.

Accompanying Enoch we made our way to the fire where, on tripods made of poles, hung huge kettles of tea and where, spread on long rustic tables decorated with wild flowers and leaves, was a feast which for variety and quantity of game, fish, and fruits, would have delighted an epicure.

Squatting down in the shade of a large spruce Enoch called his daughter and addressed some remarks to her in her mother tongue. She hastened away and soon returned with a basket of dishes and placed before each of us a plate, tin cup, knife, and fork.

"Friends," said Enoch, "I hope you have brought your appetites with you. We can serve you with almost everything except an appetite. This is our day of peace and plenty; we have roast bear, deer, moose, ducks, and wild rice, several kinds of fish, beaver, and beaver's tails, tea as you use it as well as our own Labrador tea, with maple sugar. Now, what will you have?"

Life in a Thundering Bay

The magnitude of this menu was bewildering and, as we hesitated in making our choices, Enoch relieved us of our embarrassment by saying that he would help us.

So splitting two cones of rice cakes he laid fragrant beaver's tails, smoking hot, on each and daintily placed them on our plates which he handed to us, remarking that if we did not like the beaver's tails he would provide something else. Although the pleasing excitement had put a keen edge on our appetites I must admit that my first bite was a very dainty one, but after that first bite those tails seemed to vanish like magic, they were a delicious morsel entirely different to anything that we had ever previously tasted and we now prepared to make a good meal.

I am sure that we disposed of a greater variety and larger portions of food that the demands of nature required, whilst Enoch explained to us how these beaver tails had been cooked. The tail is cut off where the skin and fur adjoin, a sharp stick inserted in the tail, which is then held over the fire until it swells up like a ball, which loosens the skin from the meat. Then a rapid pull will strip the skin off like paper. The insertion of two slits in the centre makes it ready for smoking. After this process it may be eaten at once, but, if desired, it will keep for years. The tails that we had consumed had been boiled after the smoking so that they were very tender . . . .

The next item on the program was the Caribou Dance which accompanies, and is part of, the ritual of Christening or 'The Gift of a Name'. The dance was led by Chief Centre Sky, dressed in the gorgeous ceremonial robes of an Indian Chieftain, and as he danced around all the Indians loudly yelled, "Kitchi Aiaa, Kitchi Aiaa, Centre Sky," getting more and more excited with each repetition of the honoured acclaim.

At the close of the measure, a drummer stepped out and approached me as I stood at the rim of the circle. Placing himself in front of me he commenced dancing, swinging his body from side to side, keeping time to the musical beat of his drum. Two men then approached me from behind each taking me by one of my arms. I was then told to follow the steps of the drummer for they were the steps of the dance used for the christening. After going through these steps for a few minutes the whole party lined up in single file behind me, both men and women, and with the drummer leading and my two sponsors hanging on to my arms, with the crowd following, the dance commenced.

The Chief was seated with his drum and behind him stood his choir of singers, forming a scene of brilliant splendour, particularly, the gorgeous costume composed entirely of beadwork, worn by the medicine man, was a work of art in respect of both colour and design. We danced in a circle around the lodge and after completing its circumference three times I was taken before the Medicine Man, who offered up a most impressive prayer which was followed by more singing and drumming. As the last reverberation died away an impressive silence fell on the assembly, which he broke by saying to me,

"My Dream is pleased to bless you, and gives you the name of Chief Jonia Keniu (Silver Eagle)."

I was now at liberty to watch my friend go through the same ceremony and the gathering re-formed to carry out the proceedings in precisely the same manner as for myself. As I listened to the prayers offered on his behalf, felt the throbbing roll of the drums and heard the impressive tones of the Medicine Man conferring on him the valued name of Chief Jonia Penassie (Silver Bird), I felt more deeply impressed than my nervousness had permitted me to be in my own case....

They had honoured us with the names of occupants of the air, those that live in nearest approach to their Heaven, adorned with silver, the most precious metal known to them, and they had received us and named us with the full ritual, of, perhaps, the most ancient ceremony in America and who shall say that it is not the most ancient in the whole world.

It is certain that neither of us will forget, or cease to treasure, the 'Gift of an Indian Name'. The dance went on and, although small groups would frequently leave the ring to feast and smoke, they quickly returned to rejoin the dance. Although it was late when we left for camp the fun still waxed fast and furious, with First Daughter still galloping in the lead. It had been a very tiring day for us and the peacefulness of our camp, and the distant throb of the drums soon lulled us to sleep.

Notes

[1] Just before we met up with the men, they had a harrowing encounter with Chief Blackstone, in which they suspect the Chief has tried to poison them. As a precaution, they have thrown away the food Chief Blackstone has given them, and are heading back to their camp with empty stomachs. Chief Blackstone was known to be in this area in the 1870s and 1880s. Although some sources refer to Blackstone as being Ojibway, Piper refers to him as a Sioux chief. According to Piper, Blackstone fled Minnesota after the 'Minnesota Massacres' (1862) in which clashes between the Sioux and U.S. settlers

and troops left many dead. Apparently, Blackstone crossed into Northern Ontario with his family and warriors to avoid capture by the American troops. Although the Sioux and Ojibway were traditional enemies, the Ojibway Chief Penassie granted him and his followers asylum to live around Sturgeon Lake, and hunt in the Dog Lake area.

[2] There may have been two Dog Lake effigies. The picture included here, which is from Piper's book, is clearly different than the one described by Lakehead University archaeology professor Ken Dawson in his report, 'The Kaministikwia Intaglio Dog Effigy Mound', in *Ontario Archaeology* (1966). The effigy in Dawson's report seems to have had a second head excavated in the dog's hind quarters. Otherwise, the effigy Dawson describes is also by Dog Lake, on the crest of Dog Mountain, it had been dug out to a maximum depth of 20 cm, probably filled in with white sand, and the figure was about 32 feet long by 12 feet wide. Dawson writes:

"The white dog ethnologically would suggest a Siouan origin but legends surrounding the effigy are varied. Keating [in 1834] states that it was supposed to have been made by a party of Sioux on a warlike excursion into the area. Hind [in 1857], on the other hand, suggests that it was made by the Ojibway in commemoration of the conflict between the Sioux and Ojibway which took place near the location probably sometime before 1620. This memory seems to have been kept fresh in the minds of the Ojibway inhabitants until at least the 1830s, by which time the Sioux were no longer a factor in the area. Even to this day, the Ojibway trappers in the area continue to tell stories about Dog Mountain. These suggest that the Sioux made the effigy and on their withdrawal the Ojibway destroyed its supernatural powers by excavating a second head, which might explain the peculiarities of the tail formation. Simpson, in 1847 states that, 'According to the tradition, the portage derived its name from the circumstance that two enormous dogs, having taken a nap at the top of the hill, left the impression of their figures behind them.'" [p.10]

Simpson's description suggests there were two effigies in the area, although Dawson and his team did not find a second one. The mystery continues.

death

and snowstorms

Life in a Thundering Bay

CHAPTER FIVE

Indian Legend of Loch Lomond (1906)

By Eugenie Robin

This story was first published in a local newspaper in 1906 and then republished in 1926 with the line: "A tale told of the early [18]70s told by one who heard it from the lips of the participants." It is an intriguing tale, but how true it is, we don't know. McKay, the hero of the tale, was a trader at Fort William sometime between 1821 and 1857 and is the same man for whom 'McKay's Mountain' is named, or as it is more commonly known today, 'Mount McKay'. As for his partner, Fraser, there were at least nine men with that name who worked for the Hudson's Bay Company so it is hard to know which one he was. Loch Lomond is the lake at the top of Mount McKay, which is the water reservoir for Thunder Bay South.

TLS & EAW

Life in a Thundering Bay

One night when camping at Loch Lomond, away back in the seventies [1870s], I met an Indian who had travelled from Grand Marais on a hunting trip. He was short of food, and we gave him a liberal supply also of a little eye water, which had the effect of loosening his tongue, and he told me the following story. **This story was told him by his grandfather, and must have happened at least two hundred years ago.**

McKay's Mountain, or Mount McKay, 1899

One day a party of two Indians and three squaws arrived at what is now known as Drumtochty, situated at this end of Loch Lomond. There they built their camp, which consisted of two wigwams and a storage tent made of brush. One of the squaws, a young and beautiful girl, had come with the party in search of an Indian brave named Big Wolf, who had told her that he would come back some day and marry her. At that time very few people visited Loch Lomond. The only ones outside of the Indians were a few white men belonging to the Hudson's Bay Company who had occasionally gone hunting or fishing to those inland waters. Just at this particular time two white men were camping there. Their names were Fraser and McKay. They had the Hudson's Bay flag flying from their tent pole and the Indians at once made up to them, well knowing that wherever that flag was, they would find friends. Nor were they mistaken, as the Hudson's Bay people and the Indians always worked amicably together. Well, when the Indians had made themselves known and told their story, Fraser and McKay at once told them they would help them.

It appears that the young squaw already mentioned had come a long way and was anxious to meet her lover. She had found out that he was in the vicinity somewhere and asked the white men if they had seen him. Fraser said that he thought he had seen him some days before at the other end of the Loch, where there was then a large Indian encampment.

Next morning they all embarked in canoes, and two hours afterwards were at the place designated. On inquiry for Big Wolf, they found that he was out hunting and were asked to see his squaw.

'Sun Kissed the Dawn', which was the young maiden's name, grew very pale on hearing this but concluded to see it through, and went at once to where Big Wolf's tent was located. At the tent she met a woman and one little child. McKay, who was with her, asked if Big Wolf was around, and the squaw replied no and that he went out at sunrise and would not be back till dark. McKay then asked if she was Big Wolf's squaw and she replied that she was. 'Sun Kissed the Dawn', on hearing this, turned round and went back to the canoe where her friends were and told them.

Life in a Thundering Bay

Just as she was telling her friends, Big Wolf came along and wanted her to come up to his wigwam, but the girl could not see it that way and entreated her friends to move away, but they would not go. She then applied to the white men, who immediately put their canoe into the water with the intention of taking the girl back to Fort William. Big Wolf, seeing this, got two other Indians and followed the white men, keeping out of sight all the while. The Lake happened to be very rough and Fraser and McKay concluded to stay at what is now known as the Flatt Rocks, near Carp River, through which stream they went in search of fish for supper.

While they were gone the Indians came up. They had landed in a bay nearby and found out the white men had left the girl alone beside the canoe. **Big Wolf caught the girl by the waist and flung her into the canoe, jumping in himself and bidding the others to follow.**

Just as they pushed the canoe away from the rock, McKay and Fraser sprang out from the swamp on to the rock, and McKay unslung his gun, brought it to his shoulder, and put the contents through the canoe causing it to fill up, leaving the Indians in the water. As they all could swim, and the shore was only a few yards distant, they soon got back to the rocks. Fraser jumped up and caught Big Wolf as he emerged from the Lake.

The two men struggled together but the Scotsman got the upper hand, and throwing the Indian on the ground drew his knife. Meanwhile McKay held the others up with his gun. They did not seem to want to make any trouble, and told the white men that if they were allowed to go they would go back to their encampment. Upon hearing this Big Wolf got furious, and Fraser's attention being drawn to the other Indians, Big Wolf sprang to his feet, and grasping his tomahawk, made for Fraser, and would have killed him, if McKay had not promptly shot him down.

During the fight 'Sun Kissed the Dawn' was mostly unconscious but on hearing the shot got up to her feet, and falling down in front of McKay, said some words in the Indian language which McKay could not understand, but he raised the girl to her feet and told her not to fear as Big Wolf was dead and they were going away at once.

Fraser and McKay proceeded to draw the now filled canoe from the lake, and fix it as best they could with some gum taken from the pine trees and part of the dead Indian's clothing. On reaching the other end of the Lake they camped for the night. Very early next morning 'Sun Kissed the Dawn's' friends came along and the whole party took the trail back to Fort William, where they had to stay all winter. McKay during the winter made the Indian girl his bride, and next spring, when stores were getting low, he used to take a trip up what is now known as McKay's Mountain every morning looking for supplies promised them from the east. That is how Mount McKay came to be known under its present name. McKay soon after his marriage moved with his wife to Sault Ste. Marie where many of their descendants now reside.

(Note—McKay was a free trader, living in Fort William sometime between 1821 and 1857, so the suggestion that this incident happened 'two hundred years ago' is, of course, wrong. M.J.L.B.[1])

Notes

[1] This note was added by Mary J.L. Black (1879–1939), a local historian and long-time librarian in Fort William. The Mary J. L. Black Library on Brock Street is named after her. See her research on the origin of place names in the Thunder Bay region in Chapter *Nine*.

CHAPTER SIX

The Lost Mine of Silver Islet (1922)

By Richard A. Haste

There are two good reasons why the story of Silver Islet has achieved legendary status. The first being that it was one of the richest silver mines in the world in the late 1800s, and the second, that it required near superhuman strength to access its off-shore treasures. Reading this account of the life and death of the mine gives you a new respect for the men who mined Silver Islet, and for the forces of nature that flooded its tunnels. Richard Haste, an American newspaper reporter who visited Silver Islet almost four decades after it had closed, does a superb job of recounting the mine's history, and he writes so beautifully. Where else have you heard Lake Superior described as "lithe and soft and caressing"? Allow yourself to be taken back to 1868 and try to imagine the frenzy for silver that motivated those foolhardy and brave enough, to challenge the icy waters of Lake Superior and burrow 1300 feet under the 'sea'.

TLS & EAW

Life in a Thundering Bay

In the vicinity of Lake Superior is the height of land, the great ridge pole of the roof of the continent. This region has always been a land of mystery. Here are laid the scenes of many beautiful Indian legends. The rock girt shores of the lake were the favourite walks of the Great Spirit.

Here according to the Indians, the maker of the world hid his treasures and gave them into the keeping of Missibizi, god of the sea. To this treasure land, long ago, came strange people from the south, the mound builders and the Aztecs, for copper. To this 'shining big sea water' came also in a later day, those men of iron whose deeds make up the story of the Great Lone Land, a story that has never been fully told. It is one of the hidden treasures of the lake that this story has to deal.

You who have been so fortunate as to take that most delightful of all summer journeys, the lake trip from Owen Sound or Sarnia to Port Arthur, doubtless remember Thunder Cape, that bold promontory that guards the entrance to the twin harbours of Fort William and Port Arthur. No doubt your attention was called to Isle Royale, lying to your left as you approached the Cape, and you learned perhaps some of its interesting history.

Perhaps too, if it were a clear day, the captain gave you his binocular and directed your eye to a low lying island near the North shore not far from the base of Thunder Cape, a little island that seemed not so large as your hand on which stand queer shaped buildings, now partially wrecked and rapidly going to decay, but this you will not notice, even with the glass, Silver Islet it is called.

Perhaps the captain told you of the lost mine beneath the lake, of the shafts and levels that honeycomb the rock more than a thousand feet below the level of the water, of the tons and tons of silver that lay in sight when the cold waters of the

Thunder Cape, 1919

It is one of the hidden treasures of the lake that this story has to deal.

lake 'jumped the claim' and took possession of all save the upper works. It may be that you were told also, by the natives of Port Arthur, of the dull shocks that are frequently felt, accompanied by low rumbling thunder, though the sky is clear,—the ghosts of imprisoned miners blasting for silver beneath the sea.

It was, I think, in the year of 1868 that a small party of miners prospecting for copper at the base of Thunder Cape, while surveying their claims, chanced to land on a barren rock about a mile from shore to plant observation stakes. This rock was about sixty feet across and not more than four feet above the level of the lake. It resembled the dome of a human skull just rising out of the water. Across this Skull Rock as it was then called, ran a vein of galena in which a few strokes of the pick revealed the presence of silver. A half dozen powder blasts were sufficient to detach all of the ore bearing rocks above the water line, but the vein was traceable some distance into the lake where, through the clear water, large nuggets of silver were visible. These were dislodged with crowbars, the men working up to their necks in the ice cold water. The game however was worth the candle, for the ore thus taken out, sacked and shipped to Montreal, assayed seven thousand dollars a ton pure silver.

The location was owned by the Montreal Mining Company, Limited, a company of conservative capitalists. In a way, luck had favoured them, for here within their grasp was one of the fabled treasures of the lake. As far as human laws were concerned it belonged to them. But—and it was a big but—the Great Spirit had placed it within the keeping of the sea. For three hundred miles to the east there is nothing to break the great sweep of the wind. And when, at the call of the storm, the legions of the deep come forth, the little treasure island disappears—utterly lost in the spume and froth of the breakers. Where was the man or company of men who would presume to defy these giant powers and remove this jewel from its settings?

The men composing the Montreal Mining Company were conservative. They were willing and ready in the pursuit of wealth to raze hills and tunnel mountains, they were ready to sink shafts through solid rock until they could feel the earth's internal fire. In such cases the opposition to be encountered could be measured and provided for but they shrank from measuring their strength against the unknown power of the wind and sea. Therefore they accepted an offer of $225,000.00 and transferred Silver Islet and a number of surrounding mining locations to an American syndicate headed by Alexander H. Sibley, of New York.

Here begins the active history of one of the world's most famous mines, a history more dramatic in its details than novelist ever conceived. It seems that when an unusual task is to be performed, when a Man is wanted, time and necessity with unerring instinct bring him forth. Here was a Herculean task, and the first throw of the dice turned up the man, a modest mining engineer, William B. Frue.

There is something strongly feline about Lake Superior, it is so lithe and soft and caressing. In August and September and often later, it is usually in a peculiarly gentle mood.

Like a great tiger it stretches itself in the warm sun and purrs and sleeps. It is so beautiful and seems so harmless; yet beneath this calm and gentleness you can see the giant muscles swell as the great cat extends and contracts its claws in pure enjoyment of its latent power.

On one of those perfect days, September 1, 1870, Superintendent Frue, with machinery, supplies, a crew of

**It was, I think, in the year of 1868
that a small party of miners
prospecting for copper
at the base of Thunder Cape
chanced to land on a barren
rock about a mile from shore . . .**

Silver Islet mine, 1880s

thirty men and a great raft of timber arrived at Silver Islet. There was not a ripple on the surface of the water. The basaltic ledges of Thunder Cape, even to the features of the Sleeping Giant, were duplicated in the water below. But Superintendent Frue knew the lake, he knew its moods. This one might last a day, a week, perhaps a month, but not much longer, at any rate, and then!—

There was the Skull Rock, a mere foothold, a tiny island into which the shaft must be sunk down into the bowels of the earth, while around it broke the angry waters of this 'brother of the sea'. To sink that shaft and guard it against the fury of the Lake was Superintendent Frue's task. It was finally decided to encircle the Island with a crib of timber filled with rock to break the force of the waves, while a stone and cement coffer dam was to furnish protection for the immediate mouth of the shaft. With feverish haste the work was pushed ahead, eighteen hours was a day's work. If only the cribbing could be got into place before the autumn storms began, all might be well.

One week, two weeks, a month passed and still the Great Lake slept, unconscious of or in contempt of the puny efforts of the human ants on Silver Islet.

Day after day the sun rose as out of a mirror, and sank unclouded behind the shoulders of the Sleeping Giant. Five weeks, the cribbing was done, the shaft was being sunk, and every day the precious metal was coming to the surface. Six weeks, seven weeks! The human ants were beginning to feel secure in their new abode. Then came the 26th of October. It was three o'clock in the afternoon when the wind began to blow strong from the north-east. In half an hour, the Lake right to the horizon line was white with foam.

North Shore of Lake Superior, c.1909

There is something strongly feline about Lake Superior, it is *so lithe and soft and caressing.*

Life in a Thundering Bay

Miners cabins along 'The Avenue' at Silver Islet. The General Store is on the left. c.1900

"*It's coming at last,*" said Frue, "but we are here first and I think we can stay."

When the second shift quit work at six o'clock the waves were leaping the east breakwater, deluging the men outside the coffer dam. From the rocky shore of Thunder Cape came the boom of the surf, like a rolling cannonade. The little plunging tug had arrived with the third shift wet to the skin. The cribbing on the windward side was already trembling with the impact of the waves.

Stubbornly to remain would be useless and might be suicide. It was the first trial of strength, and the result to the mind of the Superintendent was at least doubtful. Orders were therefore given to all hands to go ashore. There was little sleep for Superintendent Frue that night. He had secured the first innings, he had been given fair play, he had made the utmost score; now the sea was taking a hand in the game. All night he walked the beach, and listened guessing, as best he could the progress of the battle. How the breakers roared, how the wind howled, and shrieked as wave after wave came home!

Before sunset the wind had died down, and by ten o'clock the sea had subsided to a sullen under-swell. Frue promptly set out to the scene of the conflict, and his heart sank at what he saw. Two hundred feet of breakwater had been carried away, the cofferdam was a partial wreck, and as if in rebuke, the storm had filled the shaft to the brim with the rock of the cribbing.

The Company had agreed to give Frue a bonus of $25,000.00 in addition to his salary, on condition that before September 1, 1871, the first year of operation, he mined and shipped ore to the value of $250,000.00, an amount to cover the original purchase price and the bonus. On the morning of October 27 that bonus appeared to Frue as distant as the moon. But under the apparently crushing defeat, he lost neither heart nor his head. He had learned something from the storm. He had learned something of the game as it was to be played by his antagonist.

All hands were put to work; the cribbing was rebuilt and strengthened, the cofferdam was restored and the debris removed from the shaft. The sea remained quiet. Mining was resumed and by the last day of November [1870], when navigation closed, the plucky Superintendent had the satisfaction of knowing that $100,000.00 worth of silver ore had been shipped down the lake to Montreal. Hardly had the vessel with the last shipment got away when the mercury dropped to ten below zero. The Lake froze heavily in places, and then from the southeast came another storm.

It was a flank attack and this time the sea, as if maddened by the persistence of the invaders, brought up its artillery and hurled tons upon tons of ice against the cribbing which crumbled like an eggshell before the tremendous onslaught. But this awful battering defeated its own purpose, the accumulation of ice soon formed a breakwater against which the waves beat out their fury.

For three days and nights the storm raged, then the sea smoothed out again and Frue took stock of the ruins. The cofferdam remained but most of the cribbing was gone.

The foreman after looking over the wreck remarked: "You cannot make anything stop here," but Frue thought differently.

Nature is the greatest of engineers, and he who would oppose her must adopt her plans and be ever ready to profit by a hint.

Silver Islet Beach, c.1925. After the mine closed, Silver Islet was a popular day trip (by steamer) for residents of Port Arthur and Fort William.

The ice gorge gave Frue the key to the situation. Taking advantage of the winter and the ice he threw out a breakwater facing the southeast. The structure had a base of twenty-five feet, rose twenty feet above the surface of the water and was backed by cribbing filled with debris from the mine.

Work was prosecuted both underground and on the defences with little interruption until March 8th. Then the Lake gathered its forces for what seemed not only another assault, but the commencement of a campaign of annihilation.

Masses of ice as large as the Islet itself were hurled against the groaning fortifications which were soon driven bodily up the incline towards the centre of the Island. Wave after wave leaped the breakwaters and it seemed that the lake would at last succeed in regaining the whole of the lost territory and in driving the invaders permanently from the ground. Storm succeeded storm during the entire month, each assault more terrific than the last. There was no rest for the miners day or night. Every interval of calm was employed in repairing the breaks, and in strengthening the weak places. At last apparently defeated the great lake withdrew its forces and the Superintendent for the first time saw in his mind's eye the $25,000.00 bonus and it was not far off.

At close of the first year the cleanup showed a gross output of nearly one million dollars. The bonus was immediately paid. There seemed to be no longer any danger from the storms. From all appearances the lake had given up the contest, abandoned the treasure to the spoilers, who during the next two years took out another million in silver.

Silver Islet had become one of the wonder mines of the world. The little Island, the bare Skull Rock, had grown in the meantime to ten times its original size. It extended to the outer breakwaters and supported not only the upper works of the mine, but machine shops, storehouses, and permanent quarters for certain employees of the mine. From the eastern angle rose a lighthouse, while on the ice side were built great docks, and breakwaters for the protection of the now important shipping.

On shore a town had sprung up, a town with churches and a schoolhouse, great reducing works, clubrooms for the miners and neat cottages for the families of five hundred workmen[1]. Frue was the magician who had wrought the change. He had found a barren rock a mile from the shore of a howling wilderness, and in three years had made it the centre of one of the most important enterprises on the continent. The treasure he sought was guarded by the most powerful and treacherous of natural foes, but he met every emergency and at the end of three years was the apparent conqueror. But Nature never gives up a battle.

Ages ago, as if in sentient anticipation of what was to come, the lake had run a countermine underneath the Island. The main shaft had reached the dept of 300 feet when this countermine was struck. The imprisoned waters under the enormous pressure, leaped forth fiercely, driving the miners from level to level. Despite the work of a four inch pump the water rose at the rate of ten feet an hour. Another six inch pump was installed, but the two working day and night, could barely keep the waters below the fifth level. An order was dispatched for a pump with a twelve inch plunger, but before it could arrive the lake made one more effort to demolish the upper works.

A double attack from above and below seemed to have been planned. All previous storms were dwarfed; they were mere zephyrs, compared with the hurricane that now swept down from the north-east.

A breach was at once made in the breakwater and sixty feet of the structure carried away. Before the damage could be repaired another assault carried away 360 feet of the cribbing with the blacksmith shop and 5,000 tons of rock. So violent was the wind, that refuse rock 'flew about the island like hailstones.' Fortunately, the machinery remained intact and the pumps were kept going. At last the storm died away, the mammoth pump arrived and slowly the waters in the mine were put under control. It was a well planned attack, and the defenders won by a margin so small that an accident however slight, would have turned the scale.

It was soon after this that Superintendent Frue left the employ of the company and disappeared from its history. The fortunes of this remarkable mine for the next ten years need not be recounted. It differs but little from the history of other mines. Deeper and deeper drove the shafts, and wider and wider extended the stopes and levels. In constant fear of the sea and wind above, the work went on. Some years the output ran into hundreds of thousands. Then again it would hardly pay expenses. At last there came a year when the output came short of the operating expenses. The indications were as good as ever, but somehow the ore in hand did not seem to pan out well.

The stockholders were called upon to make up a deficit. There was grumbling and dissension. Rich ore to the value of half a million dollars was visible in the roof of the first level, but its removal had hitherto been regarded as dangerous. Now, however, plans were decided upon to put in a false roof and remove this lode.

The main shaft had now reached a depth of 1300 feet below the lake level. Gigantic pumps driven by powerful engines were kept busy holding back the insidious sea. Storms might come and wreck the upper works, but storms subside and the ravages of the sea can be repaired, but this eternal assault from beneath could be resisted only by tireless energy that never slumbered. Let the throbbing engines cease their work, let the pumps but stop for a day and the battle of years would be lost.

It was November, 1884, and the coal was running low. Only a few hundred tons remained in the sheds on the island, and the hungry furnaces would soon devour that. But more was expected any day,—the winter's supply had already left the Lower Lakes, it should be somewhere on Lake Superior now. Day followed day—it did not come. It was getting late and navigation might close at any time. Work went on as usual; some slight accident had delayed the steamer. The coal was sure to come, the miners told each other. Day and night was heard the monotonous thud, of the pumps; but all the time the coal was getting lower—lower, and the sea was waiting, waiting. It was an anxious Christmas for the folk of Silver Islet, that Christmas of 1884. There was hoping against hope for the arrival of the looked for steamer. What if it should not come? Could it come now?

The cold was intense and already the ice had formed six inches thick in the bays and the ice field was creeping out into the Lake, from which rose, like steam from a mighty caldron, huge banks of nebulous clouds.

The New Year came, January 1, 1885, and no coal. But instead there came a dog team from Duluth bearing the bitter news that a drunken captain with a cargo of a thousand tons of coal for Silver Islet had allowed his vessel to be frozen in the ice at Houghton.

The furnaces were put on half rations in the vain hope that something might happen to bring relief. But at last came a day when the fire went out, and the exultant sea reclaimed its own.

The 'Port Arthur and Silver Islet Royal Mail' by dog sled, 1883-84

Life in a Thundering Bay

Thirty-seven years have passed since that fatal day, a generation has come and gone, but no attempt has been made to fight back the sea and reopen the mine. The Island and the village that once stretched for a mile along the shore are abandoned and desolate. The great engines and hoisting houses on the island are rusting where they stood. The lighthouse has long since disappeared. The docks and breakwaters are rotting. They are at peace with the sea which in contempt has given them over to the slow torture of time. **Down in the shafts and galleries where men once worked, fishes stare with unblinking eyes at the slimy walls.**

On the mainland the great reducing plant with its batteries of stamp and vanners is rapidly going to decay. Grass and briers grow in the abandoned street **and at night hedgehogs hold high revel in the silent church and owls hoot from the rickety tower.**

Why has this mine with all its possible wealth of silver ore been left in the possession of the sea? I know not.

The old caretaker once told me strange stories of strange doings. He told me that sometimes when the air is full of light, when the wind sleeps and the placid sea reflects the great blue bowl of heaven, the surface of the Lake will suddenly heave in long, low swells and then smooth out again. Then, as from the depths of the earth, come low rumbling sounds, muffled and indistinct, like a far off cannonade. He told me, too, that at night, when the storm comes from the east and the air is filled with blinding wrack, ghostly lights flit about the treasure island, and in the lulls of the wind you can distinctly hear the rumbling of hoisting cable and the rhythmic pulsations of a ghostly engine.

I fear the years of almost uninterrupted solitude may have warped his imagination. Be that as it may, the fact remains that this silver fleece is still guarded by a dragon that never sleeps, the omniscient power of the sea.

Silver Islet, c.1902

Notes
[1] In its heyday, Silver Islet also welcomed its fair share of high society. It seems war heroes, bankers, socialites and other distinguished members of society were charmed by Silver Islet, at least during the summer months. In the booklet titled *Historic Silver Islet* (1918), Janey C. Livingstone, the daughter of John Livingstone, the government representative at Silver

Islet, recounts her memories of Silver Islet as "the cradle of social and aristocratic life" on Lake Superior. She writes:

"Silver Islet was delightful. The president's house was the centre of gaiety. Major A.H. Sibley—of Mexican and Civil War fame—the first president, with Mrs. Sibley and family; the directors and stockholders of the mine, accompanied by their families, 'their sisters and their cousins and their aunts'—with a staff of servants, spent the summer months there. Among the many notables could be mentioned the Earl and Countess of Dunraven, Ireland; the courtly and distinguished General H.H. Sibley, first governor of the State of Minnesota, a large stockholder and brother of the president, with his accomplished wife, whose influence was a potent one in the social world of St. Paul, being a daughter of the noted military commander, General James Steele, a brigadier in the war of 1812; Mr. G.H. Coe, president of the First National Bank, New York; E.B. Ward, of Detroit; Hon. R. Scott, commissioner of crown lands, Ottawa; J. Zabriskie, Detroit, and noted Harvard professors; Mr. J.J. Marvin, New York, the last president of the mine, with his charming and beautiful wife, a magnificent pianist and graduate of the Vienna conservatory, and Mrs. Marvin's pretty and attractive nieces the Misses Florence and Emma Lane of Kingston, Rhode Island, together with many others of art, military and political distinction were resident guests from time to time at this enchanting spot. A fine billiard house for the visitors, and a lovely steam yacht, the 'Silver Spray' was kept just for pleasure. Camping parties were much enjoyed, dinner parties, dances and musicals from vocalists, pianists, violinists and harpists—many of them graduates of Vienna, Leipzig and St. Petersburg, enlivened the evenings with music and song. Those were the days of the 'Kerry Dances' when life was one long holiday".

CHAPTER SEVEN

The Great Storm – Being a Recital of My Experience Beginning on 27th February, 1893, and Continuing Until March 1st

By J.C. Banks

Port Arthur, March 20, 1913

FOREWARD

Twenty years ago there raged over the Lake Superior region one of the worst storms that had occurred up to that time within the memory of man, nor since then has any storm approximated it in severity. Scores of men who were exposed to its force suffered severely from frost bites, some even so severely that they underwent operations for amputation. The hospital was filled with victims of the storm. The whole country was covered with a vast blanket of snow many feet deep. During the course of the storm the wind raged for two and a half days, driving the snow before it, blockading the roads and railroads completely so that for three days there was no communication with the outside world. Many personal adventures could be recorded. This little volume has to do with the experience of a resident of Port Arthur, who was exposed to the full force of the storm as it swept across Thunder Bay, and who on the twentieth anniversary of his rescue from certain death has caused this souvenir to be issued in commemoration of the event and in thankfulness to those who helped him back to life. To those kind friends this token is dedicated.

J.C. Banks

I read the other day of the awful experience of Capt. Scott and his brave men in the solitudes of the Antarctic, struggling against a storm that was irresistible, but ever struggling, hoping against hope, that they would be able to save their lives and in person present to the world the story of their great achievement. In a small way I can realize the sufferings endured by the men of that heroic party, for I had an experience on Thunder Bay that in some measure approximates what they passed through, though I came safely through while they paid with their lives the debt the storm demanded. God, what a man can suffer and enduring all come safely through!

The incident which forms the subject of this little souvenir volume happened twenty years ago. Those details which fastened themselves upon my memory before consciousness was blotted out are as fresh today as on the three days that the great storm continued and which claimed my horses and almost cost me my life. I had a contract to deliver a quantity of hay to Silver Islet for Captain Cross, and had taken two loads over safely. The last load was ordered to be left at Thunder

Cape. The weather was cold and the skies were clear. The sun shone throughout the day as is the wont of the Old Sol in the Thunder Bay region of Lake Superior throughout the winter months. Accordingly I anticipated no trouble when, upon returning to my home in Port Arthur on the 26th of February, 1893, I remarked to my wife: "One more trip and the job is completed; Monday will see the contract fulfilled."

I was up and had the horses fed and in harness bright and early on the Monday morning. **Although the sky was slightly hazy I had no fears,** for while occasionally a severe storm does sweep the Bay it seldom or never had happened that travel was impracticable. I left my home on the hill and on the way downtown was joined by Mr. George Benger, who remarked that the appearances seemed to indicate a snowstorm.

I gave no heed even then to the matter of storms, for the very farthest from my mind, or that of anyone else, perhaps, was the thought of what the next few hours would bring forth. Leaving the shore at the foot of Pearl Street, I guided the team along the trail I had made on the Saturday. The load consisted of seventeen bales of hay and my instructions were to unload at Thunder Cape and hoist a small flag to serve as a signal to the owner of the hay that it had been delivered. I made the gap in the breakwater and struck out across the open bay. A little way out I passed several fishermen returning to town from their 'lift', their sleighs being drawn by dog teams. I had proceeded about four miles when a puff of wind struck me in the face and almost simultaneously light snow began to fall.

I paid no attention to either wind or snow for a time, for I attached no importance to them, but I was soon to be undeceived, for the wind continued to blow even harder and harder, until from the southeast came a hurricane that caused the horses to shear from the trail in an effort to turn their tails to the storm. All trace of the old trail was blotted out and midday found us in an impenetrable swirl of snow and wind that completely obliterated all sense of direction, for not a glimpse of the land could be seen from any side. The poor horses struggled onward and by keeping their heads to the wind I knew we were travelling in the direction of the Cape, our destination.

Perhaps it was at noontime, perhaps later in the day, that I realized the futility of further struggle and decided to abandon the effort to advance.

It required no coaxing to induce the horses to cease struggle. They lowered their heads and turned their sides to the blast while I found shelter in the lee of the load. Here we remained all afternoon; I knew not where we were or how far the shore, for there was not to be seen anything but the driving sheet of snow, now torn asunder and anon lashed into an all but solid mass by the giant force of the shrieking wind.

False was the hope I had entertained that the wind would blow itself out with the day and that evening would bring the calm that usually follows a storm in this region which has its inception in the morning. When darkness fell all the furies of the wind seemed to concentrate upon one last effort to destroy us, and seizing upon the load sent the sleigh over, thus depriving me of the shelter it had afforded me.

Fortunately, I escaped being injured and at once set to work to build another shelter by placing bale upon bale, in the shape of a rude fortress. This task consumed considerable time and occupied my attention to the exhaustion of contemplating the awful scene with which I was surrounded. But there my labour was of no avail, for the storm tore the bales from my grasp and beat me down, and at last I was forced by exhaustion to desist.

The blast which had upset the sleigh was but the forerunner of many that succeeded. Through the length of the night, assault followed assault, threatening dire disaster. **And now mingled with the whistling of the winds came the ominous roaring of the ice fields** and fear came to me that even that great mass of ice formed solidly from inshore to the outer lake and from the head of the bay to its foot would break up and either claim us as victims for the waters which lay beneath or make us sport for the tossing waves and grinding masses of ice.

But there is an end to all things and the end of that first fearful night in the storm drew to a close and daylight came to allay the fears that night had engendered.

During the night the wind had shifted to the northeast, growing colder, and my clothing, which had been wet through in the soft snow which first fell and by my labours of the night before, froze to me, adding to my already overwhelming discomforts. I had neither food nor water and for long fought against the inclination to slake a consuming thirst by eating snow. Indeed, I believe I passed the second day without succumbing to the temptation and neither had I fallen before the invitation to sleep.

The morning passed and noon came and went and the afternoon brought another change in the direction of the wind. Into the north it gradually crept and keener and more searching it became. I huddled down into the snow and the poor horses stood with their tails to the storm, shivering with

Life in a Thundering Bay

Shovelling a tunnel through the snow on Cumberland Street, 1893

the bitter cold though blanketed. Even though the wind did shift from one division of the compass to another its fury seemed unabated and each change had brought yet greater sources of suffering. While I thought that I might have survived the more temperate winds from the east I realized that unless something occurred to succour me, I could not resist the freezing blasts from the north.

The temptation to sleep was almost overpowering and time upon time I struck myself in the face and pried my eyelids open to keep from doing the thing that would most certainly invite Death.

The north wind had frozen the snow and when I determined to make an effort to escape from my plight I found the task of digging the sleigh out from the six or seven feet of snow that had piled up on it almost insuperable. Possibly three hours were thus spent and even in my weakened condition I now believe that the exertion had its effect in saving my life, for had I not been thus engaged who can say that I would not have fallen asleep, never to awake.

The task partially complete, I essayed to straighten out the harness, and while thus engaged one of the horses dropped, completely exhausted, the life fairly beaten out of its body. Then I went at the work of digging again and finally had the satisfaction of exposing a part of the sleigh. This done, I tried to hitch the horse to the hind part of the sleigh and drag it out. Other hours were consumed in this effort but finally it was free of its encumbering load and then I led the horse to the front of the sleigh.

The awful cold had me in its grip and I suppose I sobbed in the impotency which had seized me. I do not know just how or what did occur, but I have a recollection of trying to back the horse to the sleigh and of feeling it tug against me and then seeing it disappear into the darkness of the early morning. Have you ever been deprived of a companion; suddenly abandoned in a wilderness; found yourself in a thick bush with the realization that you were lost; or shipwrecked alone on an uninhabited island? If you have you will realize my state of mind and the overwhelming loss I felt when I saw the last of the animal that had been my companion in the two days of awful suffering through which we had passed.

Now the law of instinct asserted itself. I must make a last determined effort to save myself.

Alone, without possible aid now that my horses had failed me, I realized that if I was to be saved it must be by my own efforts. I was unable to stand. I tried to step and fell in the snow. I struggled to my feet and again plunged face downward into the yielding snow. How many times did I try ineffectually to remain on my feet? I do not know. The snow had ceased falling during the night of Tuesday and with the first glimpse of day, I tried to get my bearings. I could not see Port Arthur, but could discern through my dimmed vision the outstanding figure of the Sleeping Giant.

Turning my back to this landmark I fell to the snow and began a ten mile journey on hands and knees toward home, that bourne which I had left three days previously in the full belief that I would be safe back it its warmth and comfort in a few hours. Slowly I crawled over the half frozen snow, now sinking into its depths and again being upheld on the hard surface of crust. The wind appeared to have moderated and I did not suffer from that cause, but as the sun drew up in the heavens and sent its glare out over the white field I felt it gnawing at the nerves of my eyes and knew that sooner or later it would mean blindness.

Desperately I crept forward, and while unable, owing to my crouching posture, to see the town I knew I was going in the right direction for the friendly Giant served as guide. As the bright sun swung around its circle and came into the west the sense of snow blindness grew upon me. My whole body cried out for nourishment, for food and water. Of food there was none, but of snow there was enough for millions of poor thirsty souls, and in the delirium which seized upon me I ate of it unsparingly and while I knew it but added to my sufferings, having once succumbed to its wiles I was unable to resist, but mouthful after mouthful I gulped gladly, thankful for the temporary relief it falsely gave.

Now, if I could only sleep all would be well. The snow just here is so soft and inviting; surely there can be no danger in so tempting a bed; I will sleep and awake refreshed, able to continue my journey home, upright as becomes a man who is soon to mingle with his fellows.

What, sleep, sleep and never wake? For the snow beds low to hold the guests who come to them. No! no! I must not sleep.

It is not night. The sun is high in the heavens and there is no time to sleep. Wait until home is reached, then sleep can come and welcome, but not here in the snow blankets of Thunder Bay.

The wind was not strong, but it had strength enough to lift light particles of snow and send them into my aching eyes and I felt the ever present temptation to close the lids and so end this source of pain. However, realizing the danger which assailed me, I struggled forward painfully, every movement causing my tortured body to send out protest, but I gave the protests as little heed as possible and goaded myself onward, every effort being weaker than the last, until exhaustion compelled me to desist.

When I tried to open my eyes after a rest of what may have been an hour but which seemed but a moment, sight had passed from them. The glare of the sun on the immaculate snow had done its work. It seems to me that I sustained a shock when this discovery came to me, but of that I do not know, for I was far gone. Instinctively I resumed my weary, body-wracking journey, nor did I know that I had turned about and was going back whence I had come.

Then from a far off came the sound of a human voice through my dazed senses, but I knew I was safe, that the hands of friends were laid upon me, that the greeting of, "All right Charlie, my boy; open your mouth," was a welcome home. Liquid trickled through my parched and swollen lips; the first that had passed them since three mornings before.

It was the voice of Walter Arnold which had fallen upon my ears and carried with the words a sense of safety. It did not take long for the rescuers to carry me to the breakwater gap, where a sleigh was in waiting, nor for the driver to land me at the Ontario Bank building, where Mr. W.H. Nelson converted his office into a temporary hospital for my special benefit, and where doctors had already arrived to minister to my sufferings. In three or four hours I was removed to the hospital where I recovered from the effects of the trying experience through which I had passed.

Reminiscences of the Great Storm

Never, in the history of the country has such a storm been known before or since. It has passed into history as the 'Great Storm'. It occurred twenty years ago and incidents connected with it are still fresh in the memory of every person who lived in Port Arthur at that time.

There was the instance of the store-dwelling which stood at the corner of Pearl and Wellington Streets. The snow was piled high on the C.P.R. track and traffic was at a standstill for two days. The company was unable to keep the tracks clear and efforts were finally abandoned until the storm ceased, for the plows were stalled in cuts and had to be shovelled out. At last a plow made its way from the east. It was one of the then new fangled rotary plows and as it sailed through the town it sent great masses of snow out upon the right of way leaving the track perfectly clear. The house referred to was in the direct line of the ejected snow, and when the rotary had passed by the front of the house had been stove in and the front room filled with snow. Two Italians occupied the house, and they ran for their lives, believing that their dwelling had been invaded by the plow itself.

One man was exposed to the fury of the storm for a few hours only and when he left the hospital he had lost both hands through amputation, for he had sustained frost bite so severe that the members could not be saved.

The street railway suspended operation for two days and parts of the system were abandoned, for it would have 'broke' the town to have shovelled the tracks clear. West Fort people were compelled to stay at home or tramp to East Fort, or find some other means of transportation. There was some talk of Fort William seizing the road under the provision of a clause which required Port Arthur to keep the road in continuous operation save for a limited period. It may be that the road was dug out in time to save proceedings along this line; at any rate no action was taken. The difference in that day and this is shown by the receipts of the railway. Then that was an entirely unprofitable section, now it is one of the most remunerative divisions. Thus time works its changes.

For a week or more the roads were blocked and untravelled. The farmers could not get about for the great depth of snow, and it was only after the lapse of a week that any attempt was made to open communication between the city and the country.

Having lost his two horses in the Great Storm, Mr. Banks was left without the means of earning a livelihood and a subscription list was opened for his benefit. One of the chief promoters and the most active agent in connection with this list was Mr. John Merrill, who was then one of the proprietors of the Algoma Hotel.

Attention is directed to a picture in another part of this little book which depicts the immense quantity of snow that piled up in Cumberland Street. All along that thoroughfare the snow was many feet deep and it became necessary to tunnel through it. Two such tunnels were made between Arthur and Lorne Streets, one of which is shown in the picture [p. 134].

One of the Cross boys, who lived at Silver Islet, made the trip from the Islet to town four days after the storm had occurred. He made shore at the King Elevator, nearly exhausted, so trying had the journey on snowshoes been.

Mr. W. F. Langworthy, the present crown attorney and city solicitor, saw on March first, his wedding day, dawn with the roads so blocked that he almost despaired of being able to make the trip across to Fort William. However, he hired several men and a team to break the road between the towns and finally reached Fort William in time to fulfill his important engagement. On the same day the C.P.R. cleared the rails of snow and trains began to run again, so that the wedding trip was begun on the day planned, though delayed a few hours. To get to the church from the bride's residence, her father, Mr. Sellers, had a gang of men shovel out a path through snow that was piled head deep. Rev. Mr. Machin went from Port Arthur with Mr. Langworthy in a sleigh, but Rev. Mr. Kerby, who was assisting in the ceremony, tramped from West Fort on snowshoes.

Navigation was very late in opening that year. The ice remained in the bay until practically the first of June. The lake fleet arrived in after being out in the lake for many days, on the 22nd or 24th of May. The Kakabeka [a steamship] left here on the last named day for Silver Islet, and when out in the ice the crew noticed the remnants of the load with which Mr. Banks started from Port Arthur on the 27th of February. When down at St. Ignace a month later, ice was seen on the shore of the lake.

Life in a Thundering Bay

thunder

Life in a Thundering Bay

CHAPTER EIGHT

The Legend of Thunder—How Thunder Bay Obtained Its Name (1887)

By Captain Walpole Roland

Have you ever wondered why Thunder Bay is called Thunder Bay? We found the answer in the strangest of places. In 1887, Captain Roland, the same Captain Roland you met in previous chapters, published 'Algoma West', a book promoting the mining potential in the Thunder Bay region. We stumbled across this dusty antique in the library. Amongst the geological information is a curious 'Note' written by Roland about how Thunder Bay obtained its name and an epic poem written by H.R.A. Pocock. In all of our years of living in Thunder Bay, we had no idea someone had written an epic poem about Thunder Bay. Pocock (1865–1941) was a British author who served in the North-West Mounted Police during the Second Riel Rebellion— which meant he came through Thunder Bay in 1885. Enjoy, we consider Pocock's poem a buried treasure come to light.

TLS & EAW

Life in a Thundering Bay

Note:—Among the most popular traditions touching the origin of this suggestive title is the following, as related in the Otchipway [Ojibway] by 'Weisaw', and very freely translated by a friend of the writer's:

"**Long years ago, while my great-great-grandfather, then a young brave, was returning with a war party from a bloody encounter with our foes (the Sioux) near Dog Mountain, a place twenty-five miles north-west of the Kaministiquia River, their attention was suddenly arrested by loud and prolonged reverberations, accompanied by vivid flashes of lightning.**

"**Ascending the heights overlooking the Kitchie Gamee, an appalling sight met their gaze—far out in the bay towards the east, where the 'Sleeping Giant' Nanabijou usually reclined on his fleecy couch, all appeared in flames, while at intervals great pinnacles or shafts of flame and black clouds were driven upwards with terrible fury.**

"Arriving at the mouth of the Kaministiquia River they were told of the fate of two hunters from a distant tribe, who, regardless of repeated warnings, provoked the fiery spirit of the great 'Thunder Eagle' by assailing its home in the cloud-capped cliff, and perished in the vain attempt to bring down a great medicine.

"Previous to the advent of the white man our storms were grander and more frequent, and only upon rare occasions indeed, could a view from a distance be obtained of the Cape or Nanabijou."

Life in a Thundering Bay

A Sketch from Port Arthur, Distant 18 Miles
W.R., 1st June, 1887

The Legend of Thunder (1887)

By Henry Roger Ashwell Pocock

Who hath seen the gentle water, breathe round the slumbering form,
And soft caressing kiss the robes of yon dread God of Storm?
In this dark land of the Otchipways, he guards the Western Gate
Towards the far lone golden plains, where parted spirits wait:
To that far land of spirits where the glorious sun burns low,
And rose and gold and amethyst about the Sun God glow!
We fathers, and our fathers saw, before the white man came,

You mighty giant heave in sleep and breathe the sulphurous flame;
Have seen him roused in anger lash these seas in furious wrath,
And all the torrents of his ire in lightning pouring forth;
Have seen him ever robed in clouds, and his extended form,
Forever clouded in his robes, his right robes of the storm;
But never saw through lifted clouds his rugged sides before
The white man came to drive away those lurid clouds of yore.
E'en now sometimes the clouds sweep down to pay their ancient court,
And from the distant spirit plains their pageantries are brought,
To robe the giant as of old and rouse him from his sleep,
Where he lies dreaming of the past and slumb'ring on the deep;
But his mighty Thunder Eagle has fled beyond the plains,
And little of his ancient state in these last days remains.

*   *   *   *

Once from the nations of the east, two wandering hunters strayed,
Their birch canoe, all patched and old, their dress of deerskin made;
I saw them in our chieftain's lodge, beside the stormy bay,
Ere they towards the setting sun should still pursue their way.
They came towards the setting sun to seek his resting place,
Where all the spirits of our dead, and all the human race,
Dwell where the sky is ever bathed in floods of sunset light,
The everlasting eventide that knows not death or night,

Life in a Thundering Bay

Or fire, or flood, or drought, or war, where winter never reigns,
To the far happy hunting grounds upon the golden plains,
And when we told them of the God, and his dread shroud of gloom,
And when they saw across the bay the clouded mountain loom,
And heard of the dread Thunder Bird whose nest was in the height,
To guard the unassailed cliffs all hid in endless night;
And heard their fate who dared to seek the nest and bring us down,
The wond'rous medicine secrets hid there on the mountain crown;
They laughed our fears to scorn and said: "Should brave men danger fear?
"And what is danger if it brings the life hereafter near?
"Now will we learn the secrets hid in Thunder's eyrie nest?
"To bless the race we leave before we pass into the west,
"We pass through sleep to Life, where throned among the hills this sun,
"Sinks wearily into his rest—his great day journey done."

Nor warning nor entreaty stayed their swift impetuous feet,
And soon they rode upon the bay with all our dainty fleet,
And journey'd on the darkened sea with measured movement slow,
A solemn cortege, as the sun's last lurid glare burned low.
We journey'd on the glassy bay, the shadowed, slumbering deep,
We journey'd with them towards the brink of their last earthly sleep.
So when the east was cold with dawn, and the lowering clouds were grey,
The shadow of the mountain loomed against the wakening day.
In earnest conclave then we prayed that Manitou should save,
The chiefs who sought among the clouds for wisdom or a grave.
The agates rattled as their boat touched light the sombre main,
The solemn thunders echoing warned, but warned the braves in vain.
With red plumes waving as they strode, they passed along the shore
To where a clouded canyon loomed through broken rocks and hoar,
And vertical the cliffs soared upon every side around,
And at the base their fragments lay, and brushwood strewed the ground;
They clambering o'er the boulders, leapt from rock to rock and climbed,

Right up amid the canyon's gloom, 'til troubled sight and mind
Had lost the tiny spots that moved along the shadows vast,
And every vestige of their forms passed into gloom at last.

   *   *   *   *

Then morning instant sank to gloom, and gloom was steeped in night,
The waters all so late at rest had crests of foaming white.
While mountain waves assailed the heaven and cyclones round us blew,
Great Manitou stooped down to guide and save each frail canoe.
The hurricanes swept by—a lull, a blast, a loud wild cry
From the rent altitudes, the towers and battlements on high,
With ancient crags crashed down the heights, and lo, each breaking wave
Screamed in his triumph round a crag and bounded o'er its grave!
The giant shook with wrath—the trees uprooted, hurled in space,
Like hails of monster spears were shot adown the mountain's face—
Against the precipice on high the wildest breakers hurl'd.
And round the whirlpool's circling deeps the broken waters swirl'd;

And who can tell the lightning's glare, recount the thunder's roar,
Or the wild shrieks that through the gloom the vengeful cyclones bore?
How long the tempests swept the bay, how long we fought for life,
How long among the lodges mourn'd the aged, child, and wife,
How long before we saw the smoke of camp fires far away,
Just where the Kaministiquia is emptied in the bay,
How long we slept and wearied lay, restored to home at last,
We could not tell; but heard the squaws relate four days were past
Since they had seen the tempests rage about the giant's bed,
And seen the seas content with heaven and mourned their braves for dead.

Full many suns were set between the darksome western height,
And still the thunder roared by day and lightning glared by night,
And still the dark cliffs towering round re-echoed loud the roar

Life in a Thundering Bay

That shook the region of the cloud, and weighed our hearts with awe.

We prayed that Manitou should aid the venturous braves' escape;
'Twas then we named this "Thunder Bay;" the mountain, "Thunder Cape."
At last when evening shadows came across the mighty lake
Fast spreading up the channel with the night time in their wake,
The night wind swept across the bay a shadowy lone canoe
That drifted slowly into sight, the wind was all her crew
And his chill breaths dying shook the tents and all the clust'ring reeds
And left the little skiff to rest among the drifted weeds,
The chieftain sent two braves to take the stranger in their care,
And when they reached the frail canoe they found a warrior there,
A warrior resting from the storms and wounded sore and cold,
With whitened hair all scathed with fire, and naked, starved, and old,
They laid him down beside the tents, and death shades like the night
Upon his face were chased away by the red sunset light.
His dim eyes opened as he spoke, but in the voice was told,
The fever spirit dwelt within; in each proud feature's mould
We saw that youth had changed to age since on the mountain side,
He dared the Thunder with his friend and every death defied.

"I see the clouds are low'ring down—I see the gathering gloom,
There are the agonies of death—This mountain is our tomb—
The rocks are shaken—and the walls of this impending chasm
Are closing on us!—Haste—Advance—Fly from this mountain's spasm!
This is the plateau—to the trees, as hail are hurled in space—
Behold the huge rocks glow with fire along the mountain's face!
The mountain is in flames! The smoke in densest volume soars
And round the crests a rain of fire from all red cloudland pours!
Lo, in this storm unaided man a thousands deaths had died—
Break Giant all the world in ruin—Avenge—Thou art defied!
—He comes! Dark Thunder though thy nest were thrice inviolate

Thou and all thine shall perish—Haste dread vulture to thy fate!
—He strikes! —and Death is near—is come—Erect thy pride my friend,
Lay down the life but not the man, for death is not the end!
—He dies! —and I die not—I go—to tell to all mankind
That man may live a thousand deaths—and deathless reigns the Mind!
By fire, by fever, or in fight, by lightning, ice, or wave,
There never sank a braver man than to this hero's grave!"

A mightier hero still then he who on the mountain died
Lay by the Kaministiquia!
        Now broadly flushed and wide
The mighty gates of evening, as the golden sun was gone,
And gorgeous across the heavens the arch of glory shone
So all the air was filled with light, and all the earth with rest,
As the brave spirit took the trail that leads towards the west.

Life in a Thundering Bay

epilogue

Life in a Thundering Bay

CHAPTER NINE

Place Names in the Vicinity of Fort William (1925)

By Mary J.L. Black

Local historian and librarian Mary J.L. Black does a superb job unravelling the many spellings and histories of place names in the Thunder Bay region. This is a daunting task, as you will see when you get to 'Kaministikwia'. Although we tend to think of Thunder Bay's history as rather recent, the place names remind us of the long history of settlement in this area. The archaeological evidence suggests the first inhabitants of Thunder Bay arrived after the glaciers melted, 7,000–9,000 years ago. Since then, the area has long been used by the Ojibway people, and many place names retain their Ojibway origins. For example, do you know why 'Dog Lake', the proverbial long weekend campsite, is called 'Dog Lake'?—if not read on (and read Chapter Four). Four hundred years ago, European explorers began to arrive; followed by missionaries, fur traders, silver miners, and homesteaders. Each group named the landscape in a different way than their predecessors, giving the Thunder Bay region its unique nomenclature.

TLS & EAW

Life in a Thundering Bay

In searching for the original Indian place names, and the meaning of the present Indian names, I am indebted to the Rev. Father V. Renaud, S.J., and to Mrs. Nellie Corbett, both of whom gave me much information, and also to Mr. John Duncan McKenzie, who checked their notes over for me. Other information I have picked up from various sources, and though I have tried to keep it authoritative, I cannot guarantee it. I give it for what it is worth, and because it is all of local interest.

Mary J. L. Black c.1910

I give it for what it is worth, and because it is all of local interest.

The city of Fort William commemorates William McGillivray, one of the leading members of the North West Fur Company, who directed the construction of the fort of the Kaministiquia River, as the company's headquarters, instead of Grand Portage in Minnesota. Apparently the move began in 1801. Building went on in 1802 and 1803. In the latter year the fort was completed, but dwellings had still to be erected.

Daniel Harmon notes that there were a thousand labouring men here in July 1805. He calls it 'The New Fort' (see Coues, *New Light on the Early History of the Great North West*, page 222). A letter from George Monk, dated Leach Lake, April 18, 1807, refers to 'Fort William'. William McGillivray succeeded Peter Pond as a partner in the North West Company about 1790; he was a member of the House of Assembly, Lower Canada, June 18, 1808 to October 2, 1809, for Montreal West; member of Legislative Council, Lower Canada, 1814–1825, October 16, on which date he died in London, England (Report, Geographic Board of Canada).

The site of Fort William was discovered by Duluth in 1679, when a trading post was established. After this was abandoned, there was nothing here until La Noue rebuilt it, or built it on the same site in 1717. This post had long been abandoned and forgotten by the time of the change from the French regime to English rule in 1763. The X.Y. Company had a post here in 1804. It is referred to by Alexander Henry, the younger. It was situated about a mile up the river from the North West Company's post. The latter post was taken over eventually by the Hudson's Bay Company, when the two companies amalgamated in 1821. The Hudson Bay Company had a depot at Point De Meuron in 1816, under Lord Selkirk.

Fort William's future was assured in 1875 (though it was not incorporated until 1892), when the first sod was turned for the

Canadian Pacific Railway. The following are the dates of the first and best known subdivisions: Blackwood addition, January, 1875; First McKellar addition, July 1875; Oliver Davidson and Co., July, 1876; First McVicar addition, January, 1885; Hudson Bay and Canadian Pacific Railway additions, February, 1890; St. Paul's addition, August, 1890; First Wiley addition, August, 1902. The first Vickers addition was registered in June, 1875, but was cancelled in May, 1879. The present Vickers addition was registered in July, 1904. (See also West Fort William.)

Algoma. Lake and lands of the Algons, or Algonquin Indians. The Indians received their first treaty from Queen Victoria in 1850. After they signed the treaty they gave up their rights and now call the district Agema-Ekaw-Oge-Baw-o-ning, meaning Queen's Landing (Mrs. Corbett). Miss Stanford says that Algoma means the Unknown, or Hidden.

Animikie. The name applied to Mount McKay, and Thunder Cape (meaning 'Thunder'), but really quite modern; it is much used by geologists, and refers to the silver-bearing formation of Lake Superior.

Assiniboin. Chippewa word 'asin' meaning 'stone', 'upwaw' meaning 'he cooks by roasting', hence, 'one who cooks by the use of stones'. (Hodge)

Athabaska. Forest Cree word, 'athap', meaning 'in succession', 'askew' meaning 'grass', hence, 'grass or reeds, here and there'. (Hodge)

Beaver Mine. Discovered in 1884, and worked for three or four years. Very rich in silver; in 2½ months $93,000 was produced in smelting ore and concentrates (Geological Survey, 1887).

Brulé Bay. Etienne Brulé reported the discovery of Lake Superior in 1618 (Parkman).

Caribou Island. Alexander Henry, the elder, in 1771, found caribou on the island.

Chippewa. An adaptation of Ojibway, meaning 'to roast till puckered up', referring to the puckered seams on their moccasions (Hodge).

De Meuron Point. Portage point for the early fur traders. The Swiss mercenaries, engaged by Lord Selkirk, wintered here in 1816. Buildings were put up by Selkirk, for the H.B.C., but were abandoned on the union of the North West Company with the Hudson Bay Co. in 1821. The De Meuron regiment was formed of Swiss, German and Piedmontese who had been forced to act as conscripts in the army of Napoleon. They subsequently served in the British army under Colonel De Meuron, and being disbanded at the close of the Peninsular War, a number of them joined the Earl of Selkirk as settlers in his new settlement in the Red River country.

An added interest, associated with Point De Meuron, is the fact that in 1872, Lord and Lady Milton spent a summer at this point, and there, was born the present seventh Earl FitzWilliam. Prior to this visit, Lord Milton had made two extensive trips through western Canada, the account of which is contained in that most interesting book, the title of which is 'The Northwest Passage by Land', by Lord Milton and Dr. Cheadle.

Dog Lake. 'Animosaigaigun' meaning 'lake shaped like a dog' (Mrs. Corbett). This lake takes its name from the huge effigy of a dog outlined in sand, which is still to be traced on the high terrace over which the portage to the lake passes. This is said by the Indians to have been left by the Sioux when they abandoned this section of the country for the west, as a lasting reminder to the Ojibway of their scorn for them (Geological Survey, No. 678). [Editor's Note: In 1857, Henry Hind wrote: "The Great Dog Mountain derives its name from a murderous conflict between the Sioux and Ojibway, which occurred some centuries since, on or near this eminence. The figure of a dog, in commeration of this event, is carved on the side of the mountain. It was nearly obliterated when Major Long passed through the country in 1823, and we could not discover it in 1857. The Sioux and Ojibway were at war when the French traders and missionaries first visited the head of Lake Superior, which event may be placed as early as the year 1620."]

Duluth City. Originally Fond du Lac. The explorer's name is frequently written Du Lhut.

Fort Frances. Named after Lady Frances Simpson, wife of Sir George Simpson.

Enterprise Mine. On Black Bay. Discovered in 1865 by Messrs. Peter and Donald McKellar.

Gargantua Cape, Harbour River. Named after Rabelais's giant, sometimes before 1760. Applied originally to a rock near the shore (Report, Can. Geog, Bd.).

Grand Portage Route. This was discovered by Jemeraye, nephew of La Verendrye, in 1731. Grand Portage, of the French and English fur traders, was primarily the designation of the long carrying place, over which baggage was taken on men's shoulders, from a point near Lake Superior to a point on the Pigeon River, nine miles distant, but it speedily became the name of the place on the lake. The situation is about 47° 58' N. Lat., 89° 39' W. Long. By U.S. charts, on Grand Portage Bay (too shallow for vessels to land, and separated by Hat Point from Wauswargoing Bay), in which is the small Grand Portage Island. The most conspicuous object in the vicinity is the hill, now called Mount Josephine, 703 feet high. The North West Co.'s establishment there, before and after 1800, was a stockaded post, 24 × 30 rods, on the edge of the bay, and under the hill; it was long a famous rendezvous of the Northmen who assembled sometimes to the number of more than a thousand. It was abandoned in 1803. The X.Y. Co.'s post was built in 1797, about 200 rods [1km] from that of the North West Co.'s, across a small stream that flows into that bay. Fort Charlotte was the N.W. Co.'s post at the other end of the portage on Pigeon River.

The Ashburton-Webster Treaty of 1842 stipulated that the route should remain common to both countries, and should be free and open; so presumably British citizens to-day would be entitled to demand the unobstructued use of the ancient trail over Grand Portage. (*Story of the Grand Portage*, by Solon J. Buck, in *Minnesota Historical Bulletin*, Feb, 1923.)

Huronian Mine, at Jack Fish Lake, near Shebandowan. Discovered in 1872 by Peter McKellar. First gold mine in this part of the country.

Kakabeka. Kakabeking bawtick, meaning 'high cliff falls' (Mrs. Corbett). According to Mr. McKenzie, it means any steep rock. Sometimes in the early records it is called Mountain Falls; for instance R.M. Ballantyne calls them by that name, and also calls them Kackakecka Falls.

Kakabeka Falls, 1870

Kaministikwia. There have been innumerable spellings for this word, and also many meanings given. Nicholas Garry, in his diary, July 1, 1821, calls it Kaministiquia [Editor's Note: this is the spelling used today], and gives as the meaning 'river of islands'. It is also said to mean the 'river that winds', and 'the river of three mouths'. I have also heard it said to mean 'the crocked squaw'. It was first known as the 'river of the Assinibiones', then as 'Trois rivieres'. Harmon, in 1805, called it Dog River. Mr. McKenzie says that the correct Indian name is Kamanstiquia, meaning 'ragged shores involving portages'. The Kaministikwia was discovered by Duluth in 1679, but the river itself was first explored by Jacques de Noyon, in 1688. In the course of time the route was forgotten, but was rediscovered in 1789 by Roderick Mackenzie of the N.W. Co.

The following are some of the forms of the word: "Kaministiquia, with some traces still of Kamanistiquia, the form Alexander Henry uses. Senator Masson prefers Kaministikia, and Kaministiquia and Kaministiqa appear on many U.S. charts. The initial 'K' varies to 'C' and 'G', and the 'Q' to 'G', and there were permutations in most of the vowels. Thus, Gamanestigouya appears in Le Verendrye's journal, 1738–39; we hear from the beginning of Camenistiquoia, of Three Rivers; Kamimistikweya is said by Pettitot to mean 'wide river'; Caministiquia is Sir A. MacKenzie's form; Harmon prints Kaminitquia; Kamanaaitiquoya appears in Malhoit; Kamanatekqoya, or 'river of Fort William', is in Keating, page 135. I have found wandering River once, and Dog River was common" (Coues, *New Light on the Great North West*).

Keewatin, means 'north wind'.

Lac des Mille Lacs. Sasagyisaigaigan, meaning 'deep lake' (Mrs. Corbett).

Lake of the Woods. The Indians called its northern portion Kamnitic Sakahagen, meaning Lake of the Woods, and Island Lake, the southern portion Pekwaonga Sakahagen, or Lake of the Sand hills. Another Indian name is translated 'White Fish Lake'. This is now applied to that portion of the lake east of Sioux Narrows. The northwest part of the lake was known as Clearwater Lake, now Clearwater Bay. Another Indian name was Minitic or Minnitite. During the French period it was variously known as Lac des Bois, Lac des Sioux, Lac des Iles, and in one case as Lac des Christineaux, a name more generally applied to Lake Winnipeg. On some maps it is called Asiniboiles.

Loch Lomond. Kasasagadadjiqegamishkag (Father Renaud). Kazazeekeegewaigamag, meaning the high lake that is always overflowing (H. Sidney Hancock).

Mission, Fort William. It was founded in 1848 by two Jesuits, Fathers Fre Miot and Jean Pierre Choni.

Mission Treaty. Concluded in 1850 by Hon. W. B. Robinson, with the chiefs of the Ojibway Indians (See H. Y. Hind's report).

Montreal Island, and River. The name appears on Popple's map in 1731.

Mount McKay. Nicholas Garry states in his diary of July 1, 1821, "This very fine mountain has no name". In 1857, however, H. Y. Hind calls it 'Mount McKay', though in the majority of references up to the later eighties [1880s], it was called 'McKay's Mountain'. It was named after a free trader, William McKay. The story goes that Trader McKay was in the habit of climbing the mountain as his daily constitutional. I have not been able to find out in what year he lived in Fort William. The Indians now call it Anamikiewakchu or Thunder Mountain, according to Mr. McKellar, or Mamanetigquia wadjew, meaning Kaministikqia Hill, according to Father Renaud, while Mrs. Corbett gives it as Missanbaing Wadjew, Crane Mountain.

Mount McKay, 1870

Mountain Road. Kichiqidijew ekahnah (Mr. McKenzie).

Mutton Island. Manisklanishi miniss (Mrs. Corbett).

Neebing. Said to mean 'summer', but of this Mr. McKenzie is doubtful.

Neebing Post Office. See West Fort William.

Neebing Township. Plan dated July 1, 1860, signed by Thos. W. Herrick.

Nepgion, or Nipigon called Annimibegon, meaning 'the lake you cannot see the end of ' (Grant's Picturesque Canada). In the early records called Alemepigon. Fort Nipigon was at the mouth of the river on the left bank about 1680. On some early maps it is called 'Fort Ancien du Sr. du L'Hut'.

Red Rock, viewed from the Nipigon River, 1870

Otter Head Cove and Island. The earliest form met with is 'Tete de l'Outre' on Popple's map, 1731 (Report, Can. Geog. Bd.).

Paipoogne. Meaning is doubtful, but I have been told that it is 'winter'. The township was laid out in 1857, and the plan signed in 1860 by T. W. Herrick. Mrs. Corbett gives 'Be-taw-be-gosing' as the present form, meaning 'double current'.

Pays Plat, a translation of the Indian name which refers to the shallow floor of the lake hereabouts. Called Bagouachi on the Moll map of 1719. (Report, Can. Geog. Bd.)

Peeping Squaw. This is a protrusion of rock which appears in the vertical face of the middle of Pie Island Mountain, at an elevation of about 300 feet. The Indian legend associates the Peeping Squaw with the Sleeping Giant, in one story telling that she, having followed him for many miles, he jumped to the Cape and then fell down exhausted, while she succeeded in getting only as far as the Pie in her jump, but that while he sleeps she remains on guard, prepared to renew her pursuit as soon as he stirs.

Pic River. Indian name meaning 'mud'. There are beds of yellow and white clay some distance up the river. It appears as 'Le Pick' on the Moll map, 1707 (Report, Can. Geog. Bd).

Pigeon River. Also called Dove River, and devises these names from the French phrase Riviere aus Tourtres, or River of Turtles, i.e., turtle doves, probably referring to the passenger pigeons. A name current earlier was Riviere aux Groseilles, also Groseilliers. Called by the Indians Neutokoagane, or Nautogonganc (See also Grand Portage).

Pithers Point, on Rainy River. De le Verendrye's nephew, La Jemeraye, built a post here in 1731, which he called 'Fort Saint Pierre'. La Verendrye described it in his journal, and said: "A fort with two gates on opposite sides. Interior length of sides, 50 feet, with two bastions. There are two main buildings each composed of two rooms with double chimneys. Around these buildings is a road seven feet wide, and in one of the bastions a storehouse and powder magazine have been made, and there is a double row of stakes 13 feet out of the ground".

Porcupine Mine discovered in 1884. In this mine was found a special mineralogical feature, in the occurrence of the carbonate of barium, or witherite, said to be the first found in Canada.

Port Arthur, called at various times 'Dawson's Landing', 'The Depot', 'The Station', and 'Prince Arthur's Landing.' Colonel Wolseley gave it the last name when landing with the troops in 1870. Changed to 'Port Arthur' in 1883.

Life in a Thundering Bay

Prince Arthur, Port Arthur's namesake, in Montreal, 1869.
He visited Port Arthur for exactly one hour (on a train stop)
in 1890.

Prince Arthur's Landing, 1870

June 30, 1886. First C.P.R. through train from the Atlantic to the Pacific during a stop in Port Arthur.

Prince's Location, on the mainland near Spar Island. Oldest mine on the Canadian shores, having been worked in 1846, or '47, when it appears to be regarded in the light of a copper rather than a silver-bearing vein.

Rabbit Mountain Mine, discovered by Oliver Daunais in 1882. Closed down in 1887.

Rainy Lake, lake of the Crists or Cristinaux (Crees') Lake. Known to the Indians as Takaminouen, and to the early French as Lac la Pluie. The first trading post of the North West Company in the Lake of the Woods district, was known as Rainy Lake House; date of construction uncertain, but John McDonnell, in 1793, writes: "In sight of the Fort of Lake la Pluie is the Kettle Falls, causing a portage. The fort stands on the top of a steep bank of the river. It was two wooden bastions in front flanking the gate."

Rainy River. Tekamimouen, or Ouchichiq River.

Royale Isle. Called Isle Minong by Fr. Dablon in the Jesuit Relations, 1671.

St. Joseph's Orphanage, established in 1870 by the Daughters of Mary, but taken over in 1885 by Sisters of St. Joseph.

Sault Ste. Marie. Named by the French in 1640 when they founded the mission of Ste. Marie du Saut. Previously it was known as Sault de Gaston, after the younger brother of Louis 13th.

Shangoinah. 'White man'.

Shebandowan, meaning long wigwam, door at both ends (Mrs. Corbett). Mr. McKenzie says that this refers to a special tent that is erected for a dancing ceremony. It is put up in the spring when the willows and poplars are pliable, the frame being made of them, bent over and woven. These are then covered with skin. The 'Shebandowan' is quite long, and the dancers enter at one end, and dance the full length, going out by the back end, and returning on the outside to the front again. It is considered quite sacred, and no liberties are allowed to be taken with an Indian's 'Shebandowan'.

The Dawson route to Red River. Station at the head of Lake Shebandowan, 1872

Shuniah, said to mean 'money' or 'silver'.

Shuniah Township, organized in 1873. It consisted of the Townships of McIntyre, McGregor, the Welcomes, Pie Island, Neebing, Paipoogne, Blake, Cronks, Pardee, and Neebing Additional. Organized in order to raise funds ($70,000 bonds) to build the railway from Port Arthur to West Fort.

Shuniah Mine, formerly Duncan Mine, discovered in 1867 by John and George McVicar; sold in 1870 for $75,000.

Silver Harbour Mine, also called the Beck Mine, discovered in 1870, closed in 1872 after extensive development.

Silver Islet, a small islet less than 90 feet square, and eight feet at its highest point; discovered on July 10, 1868, by a Mr. John Morgan, under the direction of Mr. T. MacFarlane; $3,250,000 is said to have been taken from it before it was closed down in 1884. It went to a depth of 1,230 feet and had thirteen levels. The length of one of the veins was known to be over 9,000 feet, extending from the islet over to the mainland and onto 'Morgan's Junction' a shaft beyond the Cross Fox farm. There is a romantic story of the shutting down of the mine, when it was said that it was due to the failure of the arrival of a boat in November, 1884, on which was the winter's supply of fuel. This necessitatied the closing down of the furnaces which operated the pumps, and the mine flooded. Some skeptical people think that that was only made an excuse, and that the wealth had been exhausted. Since then various attempts have been made to have the water pumped out, and the operation continued, but no great wealth has been made in these ventures.

Silver Mountain Mine, discovered in 1884, and operated with considerable success for several years.

Spar Island Mine. This was part of the old Prince's Location, one of the first mining properties worked on the lakes, operations having been carried on there in 1846 and '49.

Sleeping Giant. Many interesting stories are told in regard to this giant, and Indian superstition declares it a spot that may well be avoided.

Superior Lake. On September 2, 1665, Father Allouez entered Lake Superior and named it 'Tracy', after the Marquis de Tracy, Lieutenant-Governor of that period. Its discovery had previously been reported in 1618 by Etienne Brule. On the Jesuit maps of 1670–71, it is called 'Lac Tracy, ou Superieur', and shortly after, the second, and much more suitable name became general. Kitichigami, meaning 'great water' is the Indian word generally accepted, though that word refers to any large body of water.

Thunder Bay, Animikie wekwed. Thunder birds lived there in olden times, hence Thunder Bird Bay (Mrs. Corbett).

Thunder Bay Mine, 2½ miles northeast of the mouth of the Current River. Discovered by Mr. Peter McKellar in 1866. Developed quite extensively, and a little village sprang up. Everything was destroyed by fire in 1873, and again in 1881.

Thunder Cape, Kitchi neiashing, meaning 'great point'; also Animiki neiashi, 'Thunder Point' (Father Renaud); Kitch Naishing, 'long narrow point' (Mrs. Corbett); Animiki wadjew 'thunder hill' (Mr. McKenzie). For Animiki, see also Animikie.

Town Plot. Laid out in 1857, plan signed by T. W. Herrick in 1860.

Trowbridge Island, named after one of the Silver Islet officials, C. A. Trowbridge, Secretary of Silver Islet Company.

Wallbridge Mine, on Lot II, Paipoogne. Discovered in 1863, copper, sulphurets and galena ores. The first mining property sold in Thunder Bay.

Welcomes. Pagwassabaning (Father Renaud). Called 'the Welcomes' on Bayfield's map, 1828.

West Fort William. This section developed as the result of the construction of the C.P.R, the center of the settlement being at Brown Street, and along the river front. On the post office being opened it was called 'Fort William'. Later on, East Fort William sprang up, and there the post office was also called 'Fort William'. The west end then changed their name to 'Neebing', and in some course of time to 'Fort William, West', then to Westfort, and finally to West Fort William.

Winnipeg is Indian for 'muddy water', a name applied to Lake Winnipeg, which is turbid after a storm. Fort Garry, the H. B. Co. fort, was the nucleus of the present city. The name is first found on the title page of the 'North Wester' of February 24, 1866. The first house was built in Winnipeg in 1862.

Winnipeg River, Riviere Maurepas, Riviere Blanche, White River, and Sea River. The present name is a translation of the old Indian designation, Wi-nipi meaning turbid waters, which appears on old maps as Ouinepique, Ouinipigon, Winnipeak, and many other ways.

Index

Algoma, 160

Banks, J.C., 129
Black, M.J.L, 107, 157
Butcher's Boy, 33, 35

Calumet, 66, 76, 79, 85, 87, 94
Catholic Mission, 14, 166
Chief Blackstone, 52, 98
Chief Eagle (Enoch), 52–98
Chief Penassie, 98
C.P.R., 17, 32, 138, 141, 174
Cumberland St., 134, 140

Daunais, O., 27, 175
Dawson, K., 99, 100
DelaFosse, F.M., 16–43
Dog Lake, 56–59, 67–71, 74, 99
162
Dog Mt., 79, 99, 146, 162

Fort William, 6, 17, 107, 110
139, 141, 159–160, 179
Frue, W., 113, 116, 121–123

Grand Marais, 104
Grand Portage, 159, 163–167

Haste, R.A., 109
Hudson Bay Co., 6, 105, 159, 161

Isle Royale, 46, 110

Jackfish Bay, 39

Kakabeka Falls, 3–15, 164
Kaministiquia, 7, 17, 46, 56
146–147, 151, 159, 165
Kitchie Manitou, 74

Lake of the Woods, 166, 175
Lee, H., 42
Loch Lomond, 103–107, 166

Manitou, 66, 71, 73, 75–76
84, 89–91
Marks, T., 38, 40, 41
Mariaggi Hotel, 45
McIntyre, 6, 7, 8, 14, 177
McKellar, 6, 31, 160, 162,
164, 167, 178
McVicar, 31, 160, 177
Mount McKay, 7, 46, 103–
107, 167

Nanabijou (see Sleeping Giant)
Neebing, 169, 177, 179
Nenabushoo, 56, 71, 72, 73
74, 85, 88–91
Nipigon River, 38, 85, 169

Index

Northern Hotel, 36, 40, 41, 42 43, 45–51
Ojibway, 52–100, 146–153 157, 161, 166

Paipoogne, 170, 177, 179
Park St., 45, 46, 50
Pearl St., 42, 131
Pie Island, 46, 170, 177
Pigeon River, 163, 171
Piper, W.S., 52–100
Point de Meuron, 7, 159, 161
Port Arthur, 16–43, 110, 112 129, 131, 131, 138-141, 171–174
Port Arthur Sentinel, 22
Prince Arthur, 172
Prince Arthur's Landing, 171, 173

Queen's Hotel, 43

Rabbit Mountain, 27, 175
Red Rock, 31, 39, 169
Roland, W., 31, 45, 145

Shebandowan, 164, 176
Shuniah, 176, 177
Sibley, A., 113, 128
Silver Islet, 109–127, 130, 140, 177, 179
Sioux, 52, 56–57, 77–81, 98–100
Skull Rock, 112, 116, 122

Slate River, 7, 8
Sleeping Giant, 116, 136 146–147, 148–153, 170, 178
Superior, Lake, 4, 39, 67, 74 79, 86, 110, 113, 117, 129, 131, 160, 161, 162, 178

Thunder Bay, 4, 46, 130, 131 137, 145–153, 178, 179
Thunder Cape, 4, 5, 38, 47 69–71, 75, 80–81, 85, 110– 113, 119, 130, 152, 160 179
Thunder Eagle, 56, 75, 81 147, 149
Thunder Mt., 79, 80, 87, 167

Vickers, C., 3–15
Vickers Park, 3

Water St., 32, 33, 37, 38, 41 43, 46
Welcome Islands, 38, 46, 86 179
Winnipeg, 36, 43, 180

Bibliography

In addition to the texts listed on page 186, we also used the following books.

Arthur, E. 1987. *Simon J. Dawson, C.E.* Thunder Bay Historical Museum Society.

Dawson, K. C. A. 1966. The Kaministikwia Intaglio Dog Effigy Mound, *Ontario Archaeology*. The Ontario Archaeology Society.

Harney, R. F. 1987. *Thunder Bay's People*. Multicultural History Society of Ontario: Toronto.

MacGillivrary, G. B., 1968. *A History of Fort William and Port Arthur Newspapers from 1875*. The Bryant Press Limited: Toronto.

Mauro, J. M. 1981. *A History of Thunder Bay*. City of Thunder Bay: Thunder Bay.

For further information on Thunder Bay, also check out the excellent exhibits at the Thunder Bay Museum and the local history collection of the Thunder Bay Public Library.

Photo and Illustration Credits

Library and Archives Canada: Map of Thunder Bay (#4216), p. xiii; Kakabeka Falls (PA–022621), p. 13; The "Algoma" passing Thunder Cape (#1160), p. 47; Nipigon River (#3713), p. 85; Mount McKay (PA–028898), p. 104; Thunder Cape (PA–030306), p. 111; North Shore, Lake Superior (PA–032527), p. 117; Kakabeka Falls (#2276), p. 164; Mount McKay (#2655), p. 168; Red Rock, viewed from the Nipigon River (# 3709), p. 169; Prince Arthur (PA–147427), p. 172; Prince Arthur's Landing (#2937), p. 173; First CPR through train (PA–144822), p. 174; The Dawson route to Red River (#3012), p. 176

Souvenir View Book of the Twin Cities of Canada, Fort William and Port Arthur. 1900. Toronto: W.G. MacFarlane Publishers: McIntyre Residence, p. 7; Port Arthur Post Office, p. 23

J.C. Banks. *The Great Storm 1893*: Cumberland Street, p. 134

Minnesota Historical Association: Thunder Cape (#6913–A), p. 5

Piper, William S. 1926. *The Eagle of Thunder Cape*. New York: The Knickerbocker Press: W.S. Piper, p. 53; Dog Lake Effigy, p. 59; Chief Skeet, p. 68; Silver Islet Beach, p. 121

Port Arthur Illustrated, 1889. Supplement to the *Manitoba Colonist*, Winnipeg, Manitoba: Port Arthur Businesses, p. 28; Port Arthur Residences, p. 29

Roland, W. 1887. *Algoma West.* Toronto: Warwick and Sons: Northern Hotel Advertisement, p. 48; Engraving of Sleeping Giant, p. 148

The Ontario Library Association: an historical sketch 1900–1925: Mary J. L. Black, p. 158

Thunder Bay Historical Museum Society: Sailor's Institute (TBHMS: 983.86.62A), p. 37

Thunder Bay Public Library: Butcher's Boy (TBPL P37(5)), p. 35; Marina, Port Arthur (TBPL P233(15)), p. 40 ; Water St (TBPL), p. 41; Silver Islet (TBPL P 239), p. 118 ; Dog Team (TBPL), p. 125

Hind, Henry Y. 1860 *Narrative of the Canadian Red River Exploring Expeditions of 1857. Vol. 2.* London: Longman, Green, Longman, and Roberts: Ojibway Graves, p. 63; Falls on Dog River, p. 64 ; Dog Lake, p. 71; Sioux Dress, p. 83; Tobacco Pipes, p. 93

Collection of Tania L. Saj and Elle Warner: Port Arthur, 1884, p. 19; Silver Islet, 1880s, p. 115

Chapter Credits

1. Vickers, Catherine Moodie. Thunder Bay and the Kaministiquia a half a century ago. *The Thunder Bay Historical Society* 1924–1925, 1925–1926: 52–58.

2. DelaFosse, Fred A. Reminiscences of a Vagabond (1883–1884). *The Thunder Bay Historical Society* 1926–1927, 1927–1928: 62–75.

3. Walpole, Roland. 1887. *Algoma West*. Toronto: Warwick and Sons.

4. Piper, William S. 1926. *The Eagle of Thunder Cape*. New York: The Knickerbocker Press.

5. Robin, Eugenie. Indian Legend of Loch Lomond. *The Thunder Bay Historical Society* 1926–1927, 1927–1928: 84–86.

6. Haste, Richard, A. The Lost Mine of Silver Islet. *The Thunder Bay Historical Society* 1926–1927, 1927–1928: 36–43.

7. Banks. J. C. 1913. *The Great Storm*. Booklet.

8. Walpole, Roland. 1887. *Algoma West*. Toronto: Warwick and Sons.

9. Black, Mary, J. L. Place Names in the Vicinity of Fort William. *The Thunder Bay Historical Society* 1924–1925, 1925–1926: 12–21.

Acknowledgements

We would like to thank Dawn Kannegiesser and Lori Graham who kindly proof-read our manuscript and provided helpful comments. Thank you again to Dawn Kannegiesser for all of her encouragement throughout this project!

We would also like to thank members of our family for listening to our many stories about Thunder Bay. Thank you to Tami Saj, Cindi Saj, Glenn Warner, Kevin Scott, Dave Scott, Sara Reinikka, Jan Scott, and Ron Scott. Thank you also to Andrew Elvish and Mathieu Trudeau for many enlightening conversations about Thunder Bay, and thank you Andrew for designing such a beautiful cover. Thanks Kevin for helping us through a mountain of technical and creative queries.

We are grateful to Library and Archives Canada, Canadian Heritage, the Thunder Bay Public Library, the Thunder Bay Museum, and the Minnesota Historical Association for permission to use their images. We would also like to thank the staff at the Reference Desk of the Brodie Street Library for their help in searching out images and articles.

And of course, we are grateful to the authors whose works we included in this volume for recording their thoughts and stories about Thunder Bay all those years ago.